R. W. Werner

March 29, 1968

JOSEPH PAXTON
AND THE CRYSTAL PALACE

Joseph Paxton

AND THE CRYSTAL PALACE

A STORY BIOGRAPHY BY
Josephine Kamm

ILLUSTRATED BY FAITH JAQUES

METHUEN & CO LTD
11 NEW FETTER LANE · LONDON EC4

By the same author

FOR YOUNG PEOPLE
The Story of Mrs Pankhurst
Malaria Ross
The Story of Fanny Burney
(*Published by Methuen*)

Out of Step
Young Mother
A New Look at the Old Testament
Leaders of the People

BIOGRAPHY AND HISTORY
How Different From Us
(*a biography of Miss Buss and Miss Beale*)
Hope Deferred
Girls' education in English History
Rapiers and Battleaxes
the Women's Movement and its aftermath

*The author's thanks are due to G. F. Chadwick, Ph.D.
for his interest and help*

*The sketch by Joseph Paxton on page 80
is reproduced by kind permission
of the Victoria and Albert Museum*

First printed in 1967
© *1967 Josephine Kamm*
*Printed in Great Britain
by Ebenezer Baylis & Son Ltd
The Trinity Press, Worcester, and London*

Contents

CHAPTER ONE

Humble Beginnings

Young Joseph Paxton was always hungry. When his mother had sent him to live with his elder brother William she thought that even if he had to work hard for his keep at least he would be properly fed; but she was very much mistaken.

Joseph was her seventh child. He had been born in 1803 at a time when her husband – also named William – was trying desperately to support the family on his earnings as a farmer. William Paxton senior did not own the farm: he rented it from a rich farmer and he was never able to make ends meet. When Joseph was only a small boy William Paxton died, leaving his wife almost penniless.

It is probable that Joseph went for a short time to the village school in the Bedfordshire village where the Paxtons lived. In those days village schools taught children to read, and sometimes to write and do simple arithmetic, but very little else. Joseph was a bright boy; but his mother could not afford to keep him at school for long. Several of her sons had already become farmers, and she imagined she was doing the best thing for Joseph when she sent him to learn farming from his brother William.

William Paxton the younger was a harsh, unfeeling man. He saw no reason why his brother should not work as hard as any other boy labourer, and without any pay. It was not at all unusual for boys to work a twelve-hour day: children were made to work as soon as they were old enough to be useful. There were plenty of jobs for children on a farm. They fed and cared for the poultry and other livestock; they scared the rooks and crows from the sown fields; and by the time a boy was thirteen he might be put in charge of a two-horse plough. Many children preferred an out-door life to life in a factory or mill; and often they were well fed on home-grown produce; but they were almost always overworked and always underpaid.

On William Paxton's farm food was scarce. Like his father, he was a tenant-farmer and found it difficult to pay his way. At the end of his day's work Joseph's supper was often only a bowl of watery soup and a slice of bread. If he was lucky he might also be given one or two boiled turnips. Many years later, when Joseph had become rich and famous and was well known for his excellent dinner parties, he noticed one of his daughters turning up her nose at a dish of turnips. He very seldom spoke of the past; but on this occasion he gave his children a hint of what he had once endured. "You never know," he said, "how much nourishment there is in a turnip until you have had to live on it."

If William Paxton had been less stern and unkind Joseph might have settled down well enough. He loved the countryside and the open air and he was not afraid of hard work; for although he was small for his age he was wiry and tough. But he was an independent boy and resented injustice and tyranny. "I do my best," he told himself, "so why should I be beaten every day? I'm not an animal, but William won't treat me like a human being."

There were nights when Joseph lay awake, cold and hungry, longing for home and his mother. "But I can't go home empty-handed," he thought miserably."William won't give me a penny. He thinks he's doing enough just by letting me stay here. If only Mother knew what he was really like!" Yet Joseph was sure that even if his mother were to be told the truth there was little or nothing she could do about it. Either he must stick it out or do something drastic.

One summer's night when he had been sent supperless to bed for daring to answer his brother back Joseph decided that he had reached the end of his tether. "I'll run away," he told himself, "and nobody will be able to find me. When I've earned a bit of money I'll go home to Mother, but not before."

There was not much to do in the way of preparation. Joseph had only one suit of clothes – a shirt and a shabby pair of corduroy breeches. He put them on and tied up the rest of his belongings in a large spotted handkerchief and slung the bundle over a stick. Then, long before

9

dawn, he crept silently downstairs and out of the house. Once outside he put on his wooden-soled shoes and was on his way.

It was easy enough for Joseph to escape but not so easy for him to live, as he soon discovered. For several weeks he drifted from farm to farm, picking up odd jobs where he could and often sleeping in barns. He could manage all right during the summer, but he knew that he must find a settled job before the cold weather started. If not, he might easily freeze or starve to death, for nobody was likely to be interested in the fate of a runaway boy.

He had wandered as far as a village in Essex before he found any one willing to take him in. His new employer was a Quaker named Ford. Mr Ford was an elderly man. He was pious and stern, but he was not unjust. There was plenty of work for the boy to do about the house and garden, and there was wood to be sawn for the winter fires.

It did not take Mr Ford long to discover that Joseph had run away. "But thy mother, lad!" he cried when Joseph had explained about William. "Thy mother will fret herself to death for thee!"

Joseph looked ashamed. He had been thinking so much about earning some money before he went home that he had not given a thought to his mother's feelings.

"We must send word of thee," Mr Ford was saying. "Thy mother, boy, can she read?"

Joseph shook his head. "My mother can't read, sir," he replied, "but the parson will read a letter to her if you send one."

"I will write this very evening," said Mr Ford, "and put thy mother's mind at rest."

"I won't go back to my brother, I daren't. Can't I stay on here with you?"

"We shall see, we shall see," answered Mr Ford abruptly.

Joseph did not particularly like Mr Ford, but anything was better than being sent back to William. If his mother ordered him to return to William he would run away again, he decided. There would be nothing else for him to do.

The letter was duly written and despatched; and Joseph waited anxiously for a reply. Mr Ford grew more and more disapproving as the days went by. Several times he climbed to the attic where the boy slept at night and woke him up with the words, "Joseph, Joseph, remember thy benefactors," spoken in a sepulchral voice.

After several weeks' delay an answer came from the parson. Joseph was to return at once to Bedfordshire, he wrote, but not to his brother's farm. A job had been found for him as a garden boy in the grounds of Battlesden Park, a large house near Woburn, owned by Sir Gregory Page-Turner. If Joseph had not earned enough money to pay for his coach fares the remainder would be paid on his arrival; and the letter ended with a message of thanks to Mr Ford for all he had done for the boy.

Joseph, too, was grateful to Mr Ford, but thankful to get away from him. He was excited at the prospect of becoming a gardener, and certain that he would prefer gardening to farming. He knew, however, that unless he made good in the job he might spend the rest of his life sweeping paths and lawns and weeding the flower beds.

Although Joseph was unaware of the situation until he arrived at Battlesden, gardening was an excellent opening for an intelligent, hardworking boy. It was becoming fashionable for the wealthy owners of large estates to make collections of rare plants and seeds. There was a good deal of friendly rivalry between them; and a landowner would often send one or two of his young gardeners overseas in search of a particular plant. When an expedition returned with a collection from the tropics the atmosphere in the greenhouses had to be made to resemble as far as possible the tropical atmosphere in which the plants flourished in their own country.

Joseph Paxton was only a garden boy; but he thought that if he worked well and taught himself all he could about gardening and botany, then one day he, too, might be sent on an expedition. From the beginning he loved his work, and no job seemed dull to him. He was, in fact, a born gardener. Everything he tended grew and flourished under his care, and more than once he had the thrill of seeing a plant which had never flowered before burst into bloom. He was happy at Battlesden; but there seemed no likelihood of promotion, and he had no intention of remaining a garden boy all his life. He left Battlesden after two years and went to Woodhall, near Walton in Hertfordshire. The head gardener at Woodhall was a keen horticulturist;

and he taught the boy something of the scientific side of gardening and the elements of botany.

There was a great deal to learn; but young Paxton spent every minute of his spare time in reading and study. He was now about sixteen years old, a short, rather stocky-looking boy, with a frank and pleasant face. He was well liked by the gardeners at Walton, but they sometimes laughed at his appetite for learning. It seemed sensible enough to them that he should want to know something about horticulture; but Paxton went much further than that: he was reading books on all sorts of subjects which had nothing to do with gardening at all.

Twenty years later Paxton wrote an article in the *Magazine of Botany* which he himself had founded. It was called *Hints to Young Gardeners on Mental Improvement*; and in it he explained that a gardener who wished to be an expert in his job should be able to express himself in good English. If he wanted to write he must also read; and Paxton urged young gardeners to read good literature, poetry and philosophy as well as books on horticulture. In this way, he told them, their minds would be broadened, their lives would be enriched; and their natural gifts would be put to the best use.

In the nineteenth century "mental improvement" was taken very seriously. A man from the poorer classes who wanted to do anything but manual work could not hope to succeed without it; and the title of Paxton's article, which may sound pompous today, was considered very right and proper in his own day. His employers had no objection at all to his trying to improve his mind provided he did not neglect his work or think himself better than he was. Paxton was extremely hardworking and he was not at all conceited. But he was very ambitious. He had kept in touch with the head gardener at Battlesden; and he was nineteen when he was invited to return to Battlesden and supervise the construction of a lake in the grounds.

The making of this lake gave him a taste for engineering and an urge to try his hand at more complicated plans. Yet once the lake was finished he was just a garden boy again with no prospect of any other work. The following year, therefore, he decided to try and get a job near London, where the prospects might be better.

The Horticultural Society had recently opened their gardens at Chiswick, and Paxton thought that there might be a future for him there. He applied to the Society for a job; but as he was afraid he might be turned down because he was still so young he added two years to his age. His testimonials were good and he was offered a job: and he worked with such skill and enthusiasm that before very long he was made foreman and put in charge of the creeping plants.

Even so, he soon felt restless. The gardens at Chiswick were not so very different from the gardens at Battlesden, and his wages were very low. Would he be better off in America, he wondered, for many people thought that there was more future for an ambitious young man in the New World than in the Old. He was considering this possibility when he reached the turning point of his whole life.

The gardens of the Horticultural Society were separated only by a gate from the grounds of Chiswick House, one of the homes of the sixth Duke of Devonshire. The Duke, who had not previously taken much interest in gardens although he was the owner of vast estates, now formed the habit of strolling across to the Society's gardens. There was generally some new plant or flower to be seen; and he often stopped to have a word about it with the alert young gardener who respectfully opened and closed the gate for him.

"His Grace has been asking about you, Paxton," said Mr Sabine, the head of the gardens after one of the Duke's visits.

"Asking about me, sir?" Paxton was surprised and a little alarmed. The Duke was a great nobleman and one of the richest men in the country. "I hope his Grace hasn't complained about me," he said.

"On the contrary. The Duke wanted to know my opinion of you as a gardener. I told him you were young and untried."

Paxton looked crestfallen. He knew he was young and inexperienced but he had thought for one moment that the Duke might have been about to offer him a job.

Mr Sabine laughed. "If you're interested, Paxton," he said, "I also told the Duke that I had every confidence in you and that if he wished to offer you a post I would not hesitate to recommend you."

"Oh, thank you, sir!" cried Paxton.

"Nothing may come of it, of course; and I don't expect you would have any more freedom on one of the Duke's estates than you have here." Mr Sabine turned away. He did not want to lose the boy, but he would not stand in his way if the Duke had a better job to offer.

The Duke's offer, when it came, was staggering. It was an invitation to Paxton to become superintendent of the gardens at Chatsworth, his Derbyshire home. Chatsworth, originally an Elizabethan mansion, had been altered and enlarged by its owners through the centuries. It stood in acres of parkland on the left bank of the River Derwent.

Paxton was thunderstruck: so was Mr Sabine. "It's the chance of a lifetime, Paxton," said Mr Sabine as the two of them walked along the well-kept paths of the Chiswick Gardens, "but it won't be a bed of roses."

"It's far better than anything I could have dreamed," said Paxton excitedly, "and I'll always be grateful to you for recommending me."

"You've done pretty well for yourself, I'll admit," said Mr Sabine thoughtfully. "I hear, though, that the gardens at Chatsworth are in a shocking state. The formal gardens, the kitchen gardens and the green-houses have all been neglected for years. You'll certainly have your work cut out."

"I'm not afraid of work," answered Paxton. "And if the gardens have been neglected I shall be able to replan them instead of simply taking them over from somebody else."

"True enough!" Mr Sabine smiled down at the short, stocky figure beside him. If young Paxton had not been so capable and level-headed he would have strongly advised him to refuse a job which many more experienced men would have hesitated to accept. But there was something about Paxton which inspired confidence. The boy was modest; and yet he seemed absolutely sure of himself; and he was already becoming something of an expert on horticulture.

All the same, Mr Sabine thought it wise to give him a few words of advice. "At Chatsworth," he said, "you will have a small army of gardeners under you. Some of them will be old enough to be your father – your grandfather, even." He stopped to examine the shoots on a delicate climbing plant. "Will you be able to manage them, do you think?"

"I can only try," answered Paxton cheerfully; "and I shan't ask them to do anything *I* wouldn't do."

"You may not find the Duke easy to get on with, either," continued Mr Sabine. "He's a kind man, I'm told, but rather eccentric. He's generous, but some people say that he's hopelessly extravagant. What wages will you get, by the way?"

"Seventy pounds a year," replied Paxton.

"That's not much more than you're getting here. There's nothing extravagant about seventy pounds a year."

"I know, sir, but I shall also have a cottage. It's in the kitchen gardens, his Grace says. Besides, it's the job I mind about, not the money. The job's a responsible one with excellent prospects; and that's what matters most."

"Quite right," said Mr Sabine heartily. He went on to tell Paxton more about the Duke. "His Grace doesn't entertain very much at Chatsworth, I'm told, except for his sisters and his distant cousin Lord Burlington who is his heir, and Lord Burlington's children, of course. Lord Burlington's wife was the Duke's favourite niece; but she died very young, poor lady. It was a great grief to Lord Burlington and the Duke."

"His Grace isn't married, then?"

Mr Sabine shook his head. "I've heard that he was in love with Princess Charlotte. But the King (he was Prince Regent then) wouldn't hear of the heir to the throne marrying a Duke, however rich and well born. It had to be a prince. It *was* a prince; and now the Princess and her baby son are both dead," he added with a sigh. "Some people say that the Duke has never married because of the Princess. I don't know the truth of it, but it won't concern you. It's true, though, that his Grace is a lonely man. He's not much over thirty-five, I believe; but he's growing deaf and that cuts him off from other people. But if the Duke's life won't concern you, his deafness will. Remember to answer him clearly when he speaks to you. There's no need for me to remind you to be respectful, though, is there?"

"Oh, no, sir!" Paxton was well aware of the deference expected of the servants of a nobleman. He was going to be head of the gardens but, as he knew, he would still be merely a servant.

While he was at Battlesden it had been easy for Paxton to visit his mother and some of his brothers and sisters in Bedfordshire. It would not be so easy to reach Bedfordshire from Derbyshire; but when he went to say goodbye to his relatives before he went to Chatsworth he promised to keep in touch. It was a promise which he never forgot.

On May 8, 1826, Paxton left London and travelled by coach to Chesterfield; and from Chesterfield he made his way to Chatsworth. It was very early in the morning and no one was about when he approached the great house which stood like a palace sheltered by trees. The land behind the house had been converted into a grassy slope, and the hillside above it had been planted with trees. In front of the house a wide lawn swept down to the river; and the land across the river was also clothed in trees. There was a general air of neglect about the grounds. Paxton thought that some of the trees ought to come down; but, as he knew, he was not to be responsible for the care of the parks.

He climbed over a gate in a wall which enclosed the greenhouses and shook his head at their unkempt appearance. Then he explored the gardens, which were equally unkempt, and examined the outside of the house. When he had seen all there was to be seen he went on to the kitchen gardens which stood in the park some distance from the house and formal gardens, and he had a quick look at the cottage which he knew was to be his. Everywhere there were signs of neglect; and the moment a few sleepy looking gardeners appeared he explained who he was and set them to work.

After inspecting the ornamental fountains he decided it was time for breakfast and made his way to the kitchen quarters of the house. He was welcomed gravely and formally by Mrs Gregory, the housekeeper, a shrunken, elderly woman with bright and piercing eyes. Mrs Gregory was an important personage at Chatsworth, respected and feared by her staff. She introduced him to a tall, good looking young woman who was plainly but elegantly dressed in a full-skirted gown with a tight bodice.

"My niece, Miss Sarah Bown," said Mrs Gregory.

Paxton bowed awkwardly. Miss Bown was beautiful and dignified, he thought, far too grand to have anything to do with a gardener – even a head gardener. He was very conscious of his shabby corduroy jacket and trousers and his lack of fine manners.

Miss Bown's welcome was much more friendly than her aunt's. As they ate a substantial breakfast of ham and eggs she told him that she lived at Matlock, not far away, with her mother and her father, who was a manufacturer, and two of her sisters who were not yet married. She was often at Chatsworth, she added, and was able to do something to help her aunt. In return, Paxton told her that he had been working at Chiswick but that his home was in Bedfordshire.

Before breakfast was over the two had become friends – and more than friends. As Paxton wrote later in a *Handbook of Chatsworth* which the Duke was writing for his sisters: "I went to breakfast with poor dear Mrs Gregory and her niece. The latter fell in love with me and I with her, and thus completed my first morning's work at Chatsworth before nine o'clock."

Mrs Gregory did not altogether approve of this sudden friendship between Paxton and her niece. Sarah was higher in the social scale than Paxton; her father was prosperous, and she had £5,000 of her own – a

fortune in those days. But she was already twenty-six –
three years older than Paxton; and an unmarried
woman of twenty-six was considered something of an
old maid. Sarah was certainly beautiful; but she was
so grave and earnest that the young men she had met
had been too much in awe of her to ask her to marry
them. With Paxton it was different. After the first few
moments he was not at all afraid of her. He realized
that she had a mind well above the ordinary and would
be able to help him in all sorts of ways. He was also
deeply in love with her and quite determined to make
her his wife.

Sarah's parents, who wanted all their daughters to
marry, put no objections in the way. Paxton and Sarah
were married nine months after their first meeting; and
the marriage was a very happy one for a great many
years. It was more than a happy marriage: it was also a
partnership. Paxton had a brilliant and original mind,
although nobody as yet had done more than sense its
existence. He loved beautiful things and had a very
powerful urge to create them. Sarah was strong willed,
businesslike and extremely practical; and with her wisdom and commonsense she proved an ideal partner.

CHAPTER TWO

Changes at Chatsworth

The Duke of Devonshire was the man who first realised Paxton's brilliance. He was very pleased for his head gardener to marry the housekeeper's niece. He wanted to see Paxton happily settled; he knew that Sarah, who had been well trained in household management by her aunt, would be an asset in the great house as well as to her husband, and he had a sincere respect for her.

The Duke was quite right. Sarah Paxton was very happy in the cottage in the kitchen gardens; and she developed such a love for Chatsworth itself and such a pride in its upkeep that she began to take over some of her aunt's duties. Although Mrs Gregory remained housekeeper until her death sixteen years later, she had become old and helpless long before she died, and but for Sarah she would have had to retire.

While Sarah reorganized the house Paxton started work on the gardens which, as the Duke noted in his *Handbook*, were in very poor shape. In the kitchen garden, wrote the Duke, Paxton "found four pine houses bad; two vineries which contained eight bunches of grapes; two good peach houses and a few cucumber frames. There were no houses at all for plants, and there was nowhere a plant of later introduction than about the year 1800. There were eight rhododendrons and not one camellia."

The previous head gardener had been very neglectful; and Paxton was eager to put things right. "The twelve men with brooms in their hands on the lawns began to sweep," wrote the Duke, "the labourers to

work with activity." Changes were made in the flower gardens; and the low lying kitchen gardens were drained and replanted. By 1828 Paxton had started to experiment in new ways of growing plants under glass. The following year he was appointed head forester as well as head gardener, with responsibility for the upkeep of the parks.

The Duke was delighted with the improvements. He

had never been interested in his gardens before; but now he was fired by Paxton's enthusiasm and agreed with every fresh scheme. He was anxious to improve his own knowledge of horticulture; and it was soon an everyday occurrence for the tall and stately Duke to be seen deep in talk with his small, bustling head gardener.

With the Duke's approval Paxton made new walks, rock gardens and flower borders, and greenhouses where orchids, grapes, pineapples, bananas and other tropical fruits and plants were cultivated. He also made a pinetum – a plantation of conifers; and an arboretum – a garden devoted entirely to different varieties of trees. And he installed a number of new fountains and cascades.

These improvements cost a great deal of money; but the Duke gave Paxton a free hand and never grudged a penny of the expense. He liked Paxton immensely and was pleased to find that he was very well informed on all kinds of subjects besides gardening and forestry; and he soon formed the habit of asking his advice on every matter concerning his estates.

"You have made a great difference here," said the Duke one warm, sunny morning in the early autumn of 1832, "a very great difference. I wouldn't recognize Chatsworth as the same place."

The two men were strolling along one of the neat, well kept grassy paths; and the energetic Paxton kept darting ahead to examine the plants in the borders. "It's very good of you to say so, your Grace," said Paxton, returning at a trot.

"We must have everything shipshape by the end of

next week," continued the Duke. "I'm expecting important visitors."

"Indeed, your Grace?" Paxton was bent over a clump of bright red dahlias.

"Will these plants still be in bloom?" asked the Duke.

Paxton shook his head and straightened himself. "I have just arranged for them to be dug up," he said. "You remember last autumn, your Grace, there was a hard frost in late September which did a great deal of damage to the dahlias."

"And yet a month later we saw dahlias blooming on high ground near Sheffield. How do you account for that?"

"I don't rightly know," Paxton admitted, "but I've an idea that height and the nearness of water must make a difference." He frowned as he tried to think the matter out. "Most of our tropical flowering plants come from the high slopes of warm countries," he continued. "The flower gardens here are in a sheltered valley, and because of the river the valley is very damp. The dahlias we saw near Sheffield last year grew high up and out of reach of running water."

"You may be right, you generally are," said the Duke, who admired the careful thought which Paxton gave to every problem. "And, as we can't move the Chatsworth gardens out of the valley or drain the river we shall have to go on digging up the dahlias before the first frosts. It's a pity, though. I should have liked her Royal Highness to see them in bloom."

"Her Royal Highness, your Grace?" Paxton always sprang respectfully to attention when the Duke addressed him; and he could show no greater respect at the mention of royalty.

"Yes, Paxton. Princess Victoria, her mother the Duchess of Kent, her governess, and a whole retinue of servants have decided to honour me with an invasion of Chatsworth." The Duke gave a sigh. Chatsworth was large enough to house any number of visitors; but he disliked the pushful Duchess of Kent and dreaded the prospect of entertaining the royal party in style. "The Duchess is taking her daughter on a tour of England, staying at some of the best known estates. The Princess must be about thirteen now, I should think; and her mother evidently thinks these visits are part of the education of our future Queen. The King doesn't approve of the tour, I hear, but the Duchess is very determined."

Princess Victoria was now heir to the Throne; for her uncle, King William IV, who had succeeded his eldest brother George IV, had no heir of his own.

"October is not the best month for the gardens," the Duke was saying. "The leaves will be starting to fall, and the lawns and paths will look so untidy."

"I will make it my business to see that the gardens look tidy, your Grace," said Paxton with confidence.

"And how do you propose to do that? The Princess and the Duchess won't want to see an army of sweepers every time they set foot outside the house."

"The sweeping can be done in the early hours of the morning and finished every day long before the Princess is awake," Paxton replied. "I'll be there myself to see that the work's properly done and to take a hand if need be. With your Grace's permission I'll put a hundred men on the job. They can have time off in the day to make up for their early start."

"And what about you? Will you take a rest during the day time?"

"Oh, no, your Grace!" Paxton was shocked at the mere idea. "It wouldn't look well if I did. Besides, I'm never tired."

Paxton was certainly very strong. He could work during the day and sit up half the night reading and studying; and he looked as spry the next morning as he had done the evening before.

"Very well, then," said the Duke. "Make any arrangements you think fit. By the way, what would you suggest as a garden entertainment? We shall be expected to provide something spectacular."

Paxton's eyes shone. "Fireworks, your Grace, fireworks and illuminations! We could light up the fountains and the cascades with lamps; and the effect would be beautiful."

"A splendid idea, Paxton! Fireworks and illuminations it shall be. I leave all the arrangements to you."

The Princess thoroughly enjoyed her visit to Chatsworth. She was a tiny, pleasant looking girl, with blue eyes and a clear, healthy complexion; and she was eager to see everything that was to be seen. A large house-party had been invited to meet the royal guests; the vast dining-room had been completely redecorated for the occasion and the furniture re-upholstered. The company dined off the famous Chatsworth gold plate;

but, despite her excitement, the young Princess nearly fell asleep during her first grown-up dinner party.

Next day she was shown all over the house and wrote an admiring description of it in the journal which her mother encouraged her to keep. She was taken to see the neighbouring beauty spots, inspected a mill, watched a cricket match, and spent a day at the Duke's beautiful Elizabethan house, Hardwick Hall, on the borders of Derbyshire and Nottinghamshire. At Hardwick she wanted to inspect the ruins and climb up into what was known as the Giant's Room. "Impossible, Madam!" cried the Duke, who was terrified that she would fall and hurt herself.

Paxton had arranged for the fountains to play day and night during the Princess's visit. On the night of the grand illuminations there was a magnificent firework display; and thousands of lamps threw a shimmering radiance on the fountains and cascades. The effect, wrote the Princess primly, was "most imposing".

When she went into the gardens the morning after the illuminations the Princess found everything as neat and orderly as usual; and she was puzzled each day by the absence of autumn leaves.

"Paxton, my right-hand man sees to that, Ma'am," explained the Duke when the Princess congratulated him on the appearance of the grounds. "It was his idea that the work should be carried out at night."

The Princess, who knew that all this had been done on her behalf, was surprised and very touched. "Mr Paxton is a very capable man," she said; and the Duke agreed that he was.

The royal visit had been a particularly busy time for Paxton. Four days before the guests arrived Sarah had given birth to a daughter. The Paxtons now had four small children: a son aged four and three little daughters. With the Princess's permission the new baby was named Victoria in her honour; but the family always called her "Toey" for short.

CHAPTER THREE

In Search of Rare Plants

In the world beyond Chatsworth Paxton's name was beginning to be known. He was naturally keenly interested in the fashionable craze for plant collecting; and he egged the Duke on to re-stock his gardens and greenhouses with rare plants and fruits. In 1835 the Duke, who by this time was as enthusiastic as Paxton, financed an expedition to India. He sent one of his undergardeners, a very capable man named John Gibson, with a gift of plants and seeds from Chatsworth for the Botanic Gardens at Calcutta, and with instructions to travel in India and the Far East in search of rare orchids and other tropical plants.

Gibson's expedition was immensely successful. He returned to England in triumph with a magnificent collection, chiefly of orchids, and with the plant of a rare and beautiful tree. The tree was called *Amherstia Nobilis* – or *Splendid Amherstia*: it grew in Burma and had brilliant geranium-red flowers.

Paxton was tremendously excited when he learned that Gibson had managed to secure *Amherstia*. He rushed up to London and called at the Duke's London home, Devonshire House. The packing cases containing Gibson's collection had been delivered to Devonshire

House, and Paxton was anxious to take charge of *Amherstia* himself. At Devonshire House he met Gibson who was looking bronzed and well but anxious to get home to Chatsworth and his family. Paxton congratulated him before he left and then turned to gloat over the new treasures.

"His Grace was not up," he wrote later in a letter to Sarah, "it being then not quite nine oclock, but he was up and dressed in a minute or two, and then came the solemn introduction of him to my long cherished love the *Amherstia*."

Amherstia had been planted in soil in her packing case and looked vigorous and healthy. "I cannot detail how this important introduction took place," Paxton continued; "suffice it to say the Duke ordered his breakfast to be brought into the Painted Hall where the plant stands; and he desired me to sit down and lavish my love upon the gem while he had his breakfast by it, after which I had to be personally introduced to the remainder of the beauties, which you may be quite sure did not gratify me a little."

Paxton superintended the transport of *Amherstia* and her companions to Chatsworth. Under his care she grew tall and put out branches and leaves; but she obstinately refused to flower. The Duke and Paxton longed in vain for a glimpse of her geranium-red flowers. At first they thought that she might never bloom anywhere except in the Far East; but a few years later they were invited to see an *Amherstia* in full bloom. A plant had been sent from India to an estate in Ealing and had been successfully cultivated.

31

It took Paxton a long time to get over his disappointment at *Amherstia*'s shabby behaviour. He did far better with the orchids, however, and cultivated no fewer than eighty new varieties.

Among his other gardening triumphs was the cultivation of rhododendrons and fruit, including melons, pineapples, grapes, peaches and nectarines. One of his rhododendrons produced two hundred bunches of flowers; and he experimented successfully in the use of sewage as a fertilizer for the pineapples. Another of his successes was the cultivation of the hideous *Araucaria* – or monkey puzzle tree. Paxton did not introduce the tree into England. It was there already; but he did much to make it popular, and popular it certainly became in Victorian days.

In 1838 he organized an expedition to Canada in search of conifers. The expedition ended tragically. The two young collectors – both men from the Chatsworth estate – were drowned in a boating accident on the Columbia River. Paxton, who had himself planned their route, felt responsible for the tragedy and was deeply distressed. He was to take part in many gardening schemes in the future; but he never again sent collectors overseas.

In the meantime he had made a piece of gardening history. The Duke, who frequently asked his advice about the house as well as the grounds, encouraged him to wander freely about the rooms, and was always ready to listen to his ideas.

"Your Grace," said Paxton one morning, "I've been having a look at the wallpaper in the Chinese bedroom."

"Interesting, isn't it, that Chinese wallpaper," the Duke remarked. "I hope we shan't have to replace it for many years."

"Oh, no, your Grace! The paper's in excellent condition. It's the picture of a tree on the paper that interests me. It's some kind of dwarf banana. I've never seen it before but I'm wondering if we could grow it."

"If you can get hold of a specimen by all means try," replied the Duke. "Apart from *Amherstia* there aren't many plants which would dare to defy you!"

As the dwarf banana was shown on a Chinese wallpaper Paxton concluded that its home must be in China. After making a number of enquiries he discovered that two of the plants were being grown in a well known garden in Surrey. One of these plants was sold and sent overseas: Paxton managed to buy the other. Under his watchful eye the dwarf banana grew and flourished at Chatsworth. It was called *Musa Cavendishii* (Cavendish was the Duke's family name); and in time it produced more than a hundred delicious fruit in a season. The flavour, Paxton declared, "when in perfection combines that of the pineapple, the melon and the pear." He took cuttings from the original plant and managed to get them to fruit one after another during the season. In 1836 he was awarded the Horticultural Society's Knightian Silver Medal for his success with *Musa Cavendishii*. Later on, he superintended the introduction of the dwarf banana into Samoa, where it became a most welcome addition to the native diet.

While Paxton was making his name as a gardener he was also making a reputation as a writer on horticulture and botany. As early as 1831, when he was only twenty-eight, he had started – and edited for four years – a monthly gardening paper, the *Horticultural Register*; and three years later he founded a more ambitious journal, the *Magazine of Botany*. He wrote a number of the articles himself: they were interesting, full of valuable information, and written in clear and fluent English.

No one knows exactly how Paxton taught himself to write so well; but he was helped by his study of the best literature in the English language. He must also have been helped by his wife; for Sarah was far better educated than her husband. A man who probably gave him advice in forming his style was William Bradbury, the printer of the *Horticultural Register*. Bradbury, who became one of Paxton's closest friends, was responsible for the business side of the humorous journal, *Punch*, which first appeared in 1841 and is still very popular today. Through Bradbury Paxton met the famous authors who contributed to *Punch*; and several of these men (including Charles Dickens) became his friends for life.

The *Punch* authors may also have helped Paxton to form his style, but they had not his specialized knowledge. Some of his writings reached a wide public. His *Practical Treatise on the Cultivation of the Dahlia*, written in 1838, was translated into a number of European languages. Two years later, with the help of another friend, Dr Lindley, a well known professor of botany, he founded the *Gardeners' Chronicle*, which is still in existence and widely read today. Also with Dr Lindley he compiled a *Pocket Botanical Dictionary*, which included the history and culture of all the plants found in England.

His *Calendar of Gardening Operations* first appeared in 1842; and the volumes of the *Calendar*, together with *Paxton's Flower Garden*, which was first published in 1850, were brought up to date and reprinted several times.

Paxton was always ready to listen to advice from men who were better informed on any subject than himself. A friend who influenced him a good deal was Joseph Harrison of Birkenhead, his partner on the *Horticultural Register*. Harrison, a well known contractor, was interested in new designs for glasshouses and encouraged Paxton to experiment on his own.

People liked Paxton on sight. They found him simple and unassuming, warmhearted and wise, and with a natural dignity which enabled him to fit easily into any society. He possessed the creative urge of an artist and could fire his friends with some of his own enthusiasm. But he was not an unpractical artist: he had a powerful sense of purpose and unlimited energy. To all these qualities – and to the warmth of his personality – he owed some of his success.

He also owed a great part of his success to the Duke, who gave him unstinting help, was overjoyed by each fresh triumph, and did a very great deal to make his name known. The friendship between the Duke and Paxton grew with the many interests they shared. The Duke found Paxton so dependable that he invited him to act as his confidential agent on all matters concerning his vast estates. He also liked his company, and as time went on the two men saw more and more of one another.

The Duke of Devonshire was not only a great nobleman: he was also distinguished and highly cultured.

Paxton, with his natural intelligence and his earnest desire to improve his mind, found the company of his master of tremendous value. There was nothing he enjoyed more than a summons to the great house; no man with whom he would sooner discuss his schemes than the Duke. It was the Duke, of course, who was responsible for the friendship. As he grew older his ill health and increasing deafness caused him to withdraw more and more into his shell. When he was obliged to entertain he needed Paxton to make all the arrangements and to sit at dinner with the company; and when he was with his family or on his own he still liked to have Paxton with him. The Duke treated Paxton as an equal and a friend; but Paxton, who was devoted to the Duke, never forgot that the Duke was his master as well as his friend; never neglected to call him "your Grace"; and always behaved with the greatest deference and respect.

The Duke's sisters and his cousin Lord Burlington thoroughly approved of the friendship. Without it, as they knew, the Duke would have been a lonely, solitary man; and they liked and respected Paxton. Visitors might be surprised at first to be invited to sit at table with the Duke's agent, who never seemed to learn how to speak exactly like other people and sometimes put his aitches in the wrong place; but they were quickly won over by his warmth and natural dignity. Both the Duke and Paxton gained immensely from the friendship. In fact, it is hard to imagine how Paxton would have fared without the Duke, or the Duke without Paxton.

It was not always easy for Paxton to drop whatever he

was doing at a summons from the Duke. It would have been still more difficult if Sarah had objected. Sarah might occasionally be resentful that the Duke took up so much of her husband's free time, but to her, as to him, the Duke was the master and his orders, however inconvenient, had to be obeyed. She herself had no wish to join her husband at the great house on social occasions; and she made it clear to the Duke that she would prefer to keep in the background.

The Duke appreciated Sarah's good qualities and was endlessly generous with presents to show his appreciation. One day when Paxton was in London with his master the Duke took him in his carriage to the studio of Mr Briggs, a well known portrait painter.

"I want a portrait painted very quickly," said the Duke to Mr Briggs. "Have you time to undertake it?"

The artist bowed. "I am at liberty to do it whenever your Grace pleases," he replied obsequiously.

"This is the person I wish you to make a portrait of," said the Duke, turning to Paxton.

Paxton was thunderstruck. He had naturally assumed that the Duke wished to have his own portrait painted.

Mr Briggs was equally amazed; but he hid his surprise and asked Paxton to come to the studio for a sitting the following day.

"There, Mr Paxton, you are caught," said the Duke with a chuckle as the two men climbed into the carriage again.

"You may imagine how I felt," wrote Paxton to Sarah a day or so later, "as I had no more notion of it before his Grace said so than the Pope of Rome . . . I don't

know that you are acquainted with the name of Briggs
. . . He is considered a first-rate artist. The Duke will
have to pay £60 for it; he does none for a less sum. I am
fearful everybody will be jealous. I dare not tell any
one, and it must come out."

Sarah, though very surprised, was delighted. "Oh
dear," she wrote to her husband, "the Duke's unbounded kindness to you is unparalleled. I assure you I
was quite overcome with joy when I read it. I can easily
imagine your consternation at such an unexpected
honour. I am quite of the opinion that it will be looked
upon with many an envious eye, but never mind that,
you are the favoured one. I wonder where it will be
kept; surely I shall see it some time?" Paxton had told
her that he was not feeling well, and she was worried in
case the portrait did not do him justice. "Don't let him
make you a white face," she added, "or I am sure it
won't be like you."

The Duke had ordered the portrait for himself, and
eventually it was hung at Hardwick. It shows Paxton,
already growing rather stout, seated at a table, with a
paper in his hands, one arm resting on a book. The face
is strong yet kindly and there is a half-smile on the wide
mouth. The plump chin between the wings of a stiff
white collar rests on a black stock knotted above the
white shirtfront; and the whole portrait gives the impression of an intelligent, genial and prosperous man.

The Duke often gave individual presents to Paxton
and Sarah; and when a few years later he realized that
with their growing family the cottage in the kitchen
gardens was becoming cramped, he arranged for a new

house to be built for them nearby. This house was called Barbrook, after a stream which flowed through the grounds, and was exactly what they wanted.

At first Paxton was only summoned to attend the Duke at Chatsworth, Devonshire House, or one or other of his great houses; but in 1834 he was ordered to join his master abroad. The Duke was in Paris; and he wrote asking Paxton to join him as soon as possible and to bring with him some plants from Chatsworth, including a monkey puzzle tree which he wished to present to one of his French friends.

Paxton, who never wasted a minute of time, made the journey from Chatsworth to London and from London to Paris by coach and sailing boat. The journey took him only three days – a record for those days; and the Duke was delighted to see him so soon. He took him to see all the sights, among them the palace and gardens of Versailles with their world-famous fountains.

Paxton, who had a passion for fountains, was fascinated to see the Versailles water-works in operation. He was not nearly as impressed as he had expected to be. "Well, my love," he wrote home to Sarah, "the great day of the water-works at Versailles came off yesterday, and a grand affair it was, not so much with the water-works, which, with two or three exceptions, were not half so fine as I anticipated, but the fine Palace, the thousands and thousands of the 'ton' [the fashionable people] of Paris gave it altogether an appearance beyond description."

Next year the Duke took Paxton on a tour of some of the best known estates in England. They visited

Windsor Castle; and, as Paxton wrote to Sarah, the Duke "shewed me everything himself and took great pains to explain everything to me." Among other places they visited Woburn Abbey, not far from Paxton's old home; and Paxton informed Sarah rather smugly that the gardens were not nearly as beautiful or well kept as the gardens at Chatsworth.

He had always kept in touch with his family, with some of his brothers and sisters after his mother died. Most of them were scattered now. One brother was a well-to-do farmer not far from Woburn; another was agent on a large estate. Unfortunately, Sarah was inclined to look down on them. Her own family was more distinguished; and she did not welcome her husband's relatives at Chatsworth. This distressed Paxton very much. He had never pretended to be anything but humbly born and saw no reason to be ashamed of his family; but he could not persuade Sarah to change her mind.

The Duke and Paxton were at Clifton in Bristol when news reached them that William, Paxton's seven-year-old only son, was dangerously ill with measles. The children had not been well when Paxton left home, but Sarah had not thought it anything serious. As soon as he heard the news the Duke gave Paxton permission to hurry home; but he arrived at Chatsworth only to learn that the little boy was dead.

The Paxtons loved all their children; but William had been the best loved. Sarah never really recovered from her grief. She was too proud and too reserved to show her feelings; but very many years later, when she and her husband were both dead, her daughters found in a drawer which she had always kept locked a sad little collection of William's baby clothes. She and Paxton had another son the year after William's death. His name was George; and although he was an attractive child he grew up to cause his parents much unhappiness. Poor George was the black sheep of the family. He was hopelessly extravagant, could never keep a job, and was seldom sober. His parents adored him, especially his mother who could never bear to refuse his desperate pleas for forgiveness; and she only added to his extravagance by her frequent gifts of money.

The trouble with George was still far away in the future. Sarah, who was devoted to her children, was still more devoted to her husband. She knew that he could not refuse to go where the Duke ordered; but she longed to keep him at her side. And since, to her, Chatsworth was the most beautiful place in the world, she could not see why he should ever want to leave it even for a short time.

In 1838 she had to face a long separation.

"My love," said Paxton after breakfast one late September morning, "his Grace has sent for me to join him in Geneva."

Sarah stiffened. "Will you have to be away long?" she asked.

"Well," replied Paxton awkwardly, "as you know, the Duke expects to be away for several months. He will be making the Grand Tour, travelling for the most part in Italy, Greece and Turkey."

"And his Grace expects you to travel with him?" Sarah gave a hopeless sigh.

"That is his idea. He's got used to having me around to smooth out all the little difficulties."

"But won't he have a courier?"

"Of course he will. No gentleman would dream of visiting distant parts without a courier. He will have a doctor with him too as well as the servants."

Sarah leaned her elbows on the breakfast table and rested her chin in her hands. "Does he really need you as well, then?" she asked, with tears in her eyes. "Chatsworth looks so lovely in the autumn, and the men are already starting work on the Great Stove."

"I know, I know, my love," Paxton said sympathetically. "I hate to leave you and the children, and you with another baby on the way. I don't want to leave the Great Stove, either."

The Great Stove (or Conservatory) was Paxton's latest scheme. For some years he had been experimenting in improvements in greenhouse design. The usual greenhouse of the time was a clumsy affair which did not do its work properly. It generally had a sloping roof made of coarse, opaque glass set in a heavy wooden framework with sash-bars and rafters which excluded most of the light. As early as 1828 Paxton had experimented with lighter sash-bars which admitted more light. In some cases metal was used for roofing in place of wood; but, as Paxton found, metal was expensive. It had another fault. It could not be made entirely watertight and always leaked; and greenhouses with metal roofs were too cold for the plants in winter and too hot in summer.

Paxton then tried using more glass and less wood. He ordered sheets of large, clear glass; and his greenhouses were made with sliding sides which could be opened at any given point. He also began to design roofs on what is known as the ridge-and-furrow (or ridge-and-valley) principle, using parallel glass rows of the letter V in the valleys. Some of these roofs were flat; others were curving; and the curved roofs seemed to give the best results.

In order to get rid of the heavy framework Paxton began to experiment with slender iron columns as supports for the roof. These were hollowed out to take lead water pipes; they were joined at the top to gutters, and so served both to reinforce the roof and act as drains. Paxton had the floors of his greenhouses made of wooden slats, through which dust could easily be swept; and, to help with the making of sash-bars, he started experimenting with a machine which cut grooves to carry glass panes and which was connected with a small steam-engine.

The idea for the Great Stove grew naturally out of his earlier experiments. It was to be a huge building – the largest glasshouse in the world – with a ridge-and-furrow roof. It was to be 277 feet in length, 123 feet broad, and would have a wide central aisle and side aisles. At its highest point the curving roof would be 67 feet from the ground; and when finished the conservatory would be stocked with all sorts of tropical trees and plants.

Paxton was neither an architect nor an engineer; and so he had studied the work of other men who were working in metal, wood and glass. But the idea and the design for the Great Stove were his own; and he had no wish to leave the building for more than a brief time.

"Who will take charge while you are away?" Sarah was asking. She would have given much to keep her husband at home; but, as always, she had accepted the Duke's word as law.

"Andrews, as head gardener under me, will see to the gardens. He's an excellent fellow and we can trust him absolutely. I've had my eye on him for a long time and he certainly earned his promotion. As for the estate work, I know I can rely on you to see that nothing goes wrong and to report to me anything you see fit. I shall leave exact instructions as to how work on the Great Stove is to proceed; and I am sure you will keep everybody up to the mark. I rely entirely on your good sense and judgment."

"Of course you can rely on me to do my best," replied Sarah warmly. Then she sighed again. "If only you had agreed to take charge of the gardens at Windsor Castle!"

"My dear, you know that was impossible. I could never leave the Duke after all he has done for me. Besides, you would have hated to leave Barbrook and Chatsworth."

"Indeed I should," admitted Sarah. "But the Queen wouldn't have sent for you to go on the Grand Tour and so at least I could have had you with me."

"It was quite out of the question," said Paxton

firmly. While on a visit to Windsor earlier in the year he had been told that the head gardener was retiring and that the post could be his for the asking. This was his second visit to the gardens at Windsor. On the first occasion he had accompanied the Duke as his agent. This time he went as a member of a three-man Commission of expert gardeners. The Commission had been set up by the Treasury to enquire into the management of the royal gardens, particularly the gardens at Kew. The Commission found that Kew Gardens were shamefully neglected and strongly advised that they should be cared for and preserved for the nation; and so indeed they were. To Paxton's surprise the gardens at Windsor were equally neglected. To have accepted the post of head gardener would have been a great opportunity; but Paxton turned down the idea after only a moment's hesitation. His loyalty was to the Duke; and, as he knew very well, neither at Windsor nor anywhere else would he be given the same freedom to do as he liked.

"Well," said Sarah more briskly, "as we're not at Windsor I suppose I must go and see about your outfit for foreign parts." She turned to give her husband a forgiving kiss. "You will take care of yourself, won't you? I don't trust the foreign climate, and I've heard that the Turks in particular are a very treacherous people."

"I shall take care of myself, never fear," said Paxton. Then he added with feeling: "I could do nothing without you, Sarah, nothing at all."

He was not exaggerating. If he had married an ordinary woman he could not have given her so much responsibility; but he was confident – and the Duke was also confident – that under her care nothing would go wrong at Chatsworth while they were away.

Sarah was lonely and rather scared without her husband, fearful that he would be taken ill when she was not there to nurse him. Despite his broad, stocky frame and healthy appearance he was not robust; and Sarah worried because he drove himself too hard. But there was nothing she could do about it except implore him in her letters to take the greatest care. She wrote to him frequently while he was away and expected a reply to every letter. This was not easy when he was busy or overworked; but he promised he would write often and he kept his word.

His first letter, dated October 2, 1838, came from Geneva.

My dear love, you will be delighted to hear that I have reached this enchanting place in safety after a journey of three nights and three and a half days from Paris in the Diligence [stage coach], which never stopped except twenty minutes each morning and evening for us to get a little something to eat.

Well, I have so much to say and tell you that I hardly know which end to begin first. I am almost like a steam boiler with the safety valve closed, ready to burst; and to tell you anything of the country I have passed, with the events and observations I have made, would occupy an Encyclopaedia at least six inches thick. Don't laugh; it is a fact . . . The Duke received me most kindly. He was more than astonished at the rapidity of my journey. He was pleased to say that no one but I could have done it in the time. His Grace has been in a terrible stew for want of me for some time. He would reserve some of the grand sights of Switzerland until I came, and they all say how he has worried himself. I am now to be the grand leader of the band until all the grand sights are exhausted ...

Many of Paxton's letters contained messages to the children – two-year-old George and his elder sisters, Emily who was eleven, Blanche, seven, and Victoria, five. "*Emily*," he wrote in one letter, "I hope you are of great use to your Mother every Saturday, when you come home from school, and that you attend well to your music. I shall bring you home something from these beautiful countries that I am sure will please; therefore pray be a good child. *Blanche*: Pray remember me sometimes, and be kind to your sisters and brother. I will bring you some pretty things as well as Emily. *Victoria*: I hope you are a nice little girl and do what your mother says to you. I shall also bring you some pretty things. *Georgey:* Scold them all well if they are naughty and give your mother a kiss to send me in her next letter."

Paxton thoroughly enjoyed buying presents for his family and never returned home empty-handed. "I have brought some nice things," he wrote to Sarah from Rome. "I shall not tell you what they are until you see them, but I feel sure you will like them." He had just received a letter with the long awaited news of the birth of Sarah's baby. "The account you give of my little new daughter," he wrote, "is very satisfactory. The Duke asked me the reason why we had so many girls," he added; and, although he did his best to hide it, he was disappointed that Laura, the new baby, was not a boy. George remained the only boy; and the Paxton family was later completed with the arrival of two more girls – Rosa and Annie.

As soon as Paxton had joined him the Duke began to relax and enjoy the Grand Tour. Paxton could be relied on to smooth out all the difficulties of foreign travel: bully the courier, who did not appear to be the slightest use; and look after the servants. A young doctor named Condell had also joined the party at Geneva. He was to be the Duke's personal doctor for the rest of his life, and became one of Paxton's close friends.

The Duke liked Paxton to travel with him in his own carriage. The two men had plenty to talk about; and the Duke could point out the various sights and beauty spots to an appreciative observer. Occasionally, however, Paxton proved inattentive. "A little bored," wrote the Duke fretfully in his diary, "for Mr P. sleeps and ruminates sometimes when I wish to converse, but he is everything for me."

It is not surprising that Paxton occasionally dropped off to sleep as the Duke's retinue of carriages rumbled and swayed across Europe. He had to make all the arrangements, for the Duke relied on him completely. The party rose at five o'clock or even earlier each morning and were on the move until seven or eight in the evening. "The Duke is a most excellent getter-up," wrote Paxton to Sarah. He could not resist boasting a little of his own efficiency and his influence with his master. "I have kept him in excellent humour," he added, "much to the satisfaction of all about him. I understand he was so cross before I came that the people were about to petition him to read prayers in the morning!!!"

Paxton was thoroughly enjoying himself. He had a natural love for beautiful scenery and works of art; and he was particularly delighted with Italy. The Duke, who knew a great deal about painting and sculpture, explained everything to him and so added immensely to his knowledge and appreciation.

In Rome, where the Duke spent £1,000 buying works of art for one or other of his houses, Paxton spent some of his own money. "I have almost ruined myself here in buying things today," he confessed to Sarah. "I have given £38 for two objects that I fell desperately in love with two days after we came here. I am sure you will like them, for no soul can look upon them without delight. I have spent very near a hundred pounds here on various things . . . You will perhaps say I am foolish to spend so much money. It may be so, but remember I shall never see Rome again."

The Duke, of course, was very generous with presents. He was also helping Paxton to learn Italian. Paxton was an apt pupil. In February, 1839, he wrote to Sarah from Naples: "I have got on so well . . . that I can go anywhere alone, buy anything, and ask all sorts of questions with perfect ease. If I was to remain in the country three months longer I should speak the language as well as a native."

There were a number of places still to visit; and wherever they stayed Paxton anxiously awaited Sarah's budget of news from Chatsworth. The elder children, wrote Sarah, missed their father badly, never stopped talking about him, and had cried every day since he left. It is possible that Sarah, who missed her husband unbearably, may have encouraged the children's tears by weeping herself. In any event the whole family was longing for his return. News from the estate was good. "*Amherstia* is making another growth," wrote Sarah, for the Duke and Paxton were still expecting the tree to flower; "there are twenty-five lovely blossoms in the orchid house; the parsonage house is being furnished . . . The boiler has come for the Great Conservatory . . . The south front at Chatsworth is looking gorgeous now the window frames are gilt outside; two men and two women are putting up silk in the drawing-room, everything goes on well with the Conservatory, the foremen have completed the plan of work left [by you] and must now start afresh – the intermediate ribs will be ready in a fortnight and glazing will then begin."

Paxton himself was quite ready to go home. Sarah needed him, and he was worried in case anything went wrong with the building of the Conservatory. But the Duke had set his heart on showing him Malta, Greece and Constantinople; and Paxton, who could not very well refuse, was also glad of the chance to see more of the world. "I pray daily for you all," he wrote from Athens, "and as the distance between us becomes greater my thoughts are more often directed to Chatsworth . . . I am grieved to think how worried you must be by my not being at home this spring. I don't see any probability now of my reaching home before May." He begged Sarah to continue sending him detailed reports and to keep everybody on the estate up to the mark. "Have everything ready for me to decide when I come home," he said. Among other things, he asked her to see about having plans drawn up for a couple of new cottages on the estate; for work to be completed in the Arboretum; and, above all, to keep a close watch on the progress of the Great Conservatory. Sarah was perfectly equal to this task; and she carried it out as few other women could have done. Without her help Paxton might well have returned to find things at a standstill, certainly as far as the Conservatory was concerned.

"You will think I shall never return again," he wrote

from Constantinople at the end of March; "but I believe you will have no cause in the end to regret my long journey, for my health is so well established that I hardly feel the same person. My dear children would not know me if they were to see me now. I wear a Greek cap and Italian cloak something like this, with long flowing hair," he added, with a drawing to illustrate his appearance; "but I will modernize myself before I come home. I hope the dear little creatures are all well. I long much, very much, to hear all their little prattles again, and to see you all placed round a happy table."

He left for home in mid-April when the Duke returned to Naples. He brought with him a great many packing cases filled with treasures which the Duke had bought and three dozen orange trees from Malta.

The journey took several weeks; but in May there was a grand family reunion. The children hugged and kissed their father; and Sarah was thankful to have him home once more, and looking so sunburned and well. "The poor little children laughed, cried, and laughed again, all in a breath," wrote Paxton to the Duke; and he set to work to unpack the presents he had bought for them and their mother. He was delighted to be home, but he could not help wondering how the Duke was managing without him. He was very well aware how fortunate he had been to have seen so much of the world and realized how much he had gained from the experience.

"I beg your Grace will accept my sincere thanks for the great kindness which I have so bountifully received at your hands on all occasions," he wrote, "and particularly for the delightful tour which I have so recently made, and which has so much improved my mind in many respects. I looked through the Sculpture Gallery [at Chatsworth] and the pictures and sketches with quite new eyes. I saw a thousand beauties in them which I had not appreciated before."

CHAPTER FOUR

The Great Conservatory and the Lily House

The Great Conservatory took three years to build. Paxton had planned it so that it stood some distance from the house and was hidden by trees; and a special clearing had been made for it in the midst of a wood. It was completed with the help of Paxton's invention, the sash-bar machine. This machine had first been used for grooving sash-bars to carry glass panes: now Paxton had perfected it so that it made the sash-bars completely. In 1840 he was awarded the Silver Medal of the Royal Society of Arts for the invention.

When finished the Conservatory was planted with a magnificent collection of trees, flowering shrubs and rare tropical plants. The central aisle was so wide that the Duke could drive through it in his carriage and pair; and it had a winding staircase, hidden by rocks, to a gallery from which visitors could look down on the scene below.

People flocked to see this new marvel – the largest and most splendid glasshouse in the world, they were told. The Duke kept a coach always ready to transport his guests to and fro; and at night when it was illuminated it looked like some vast fairy palace.

The Duke was overjoyed. "The Conservatory is glorious," he gloated, "and my plants – how lovely they will look in it." People were amazed and over-awed by the building. One enthusiastic guest went as far as to declare that after St Peter's in Rome the Great Conservatory was the finest building in the world. This was a wild

over-statement; but many other people were almost as enthusiastic.

An enormous amount of money was needed for the building and upkeep of the Great Conservatory; but the Duke considered it money well spent. He was as elated as Paxton by all the praise; for, after all, he had discovered Paxton and helped him all along the way; and now people were calling his discovery a genius.

Among other schemes on which Paxton was engaged

at the time was the creation of a massive set of artificial rockworks on a piece of sloping ground near the Conservatory. The separate boulders, carefully cemented together, were piled one on the other in a heavy, overhanging structure. The Duke was especially impressed by this feat. As he wrote in his Handbook: "The spirit of some Druid seems to animate Mr Paxton in these bulky removals." Today, with the outlines of the great boulders softened by more than a hundred years' growth of vegetation, it is almost impossible to tell that the rockworks were not originally a natural formation.

Paxton was also designing houses. At the Duke's request he rebuilt the village of Edensor which stood on the Chatsworth estate near the entrance to the park. He had started work in 1838 by moving the tenants to temporary homes in other villages on the estate; and his designs were modern and imaginative. By 1840 he had the help of a trained architectural assistant, John Robertson, but he was the guiding spirit. The new houses were grouped in a sheltered valley concealed from the great house. They were comfortable and roomy, and each was supplied with piped water – something most unusual in those days in the houses of the poor. Behind the houses there were fields where cows could graze. There was also a village school, a public playground, and a number of other improvements which showed Paxton's continuing concern for the needs of the poor. Edensor, which was finished in 1842, was one of the first of the new "model" villages.

At about the same time the Duke asked Paxton to

alter and extend Bolton Abbey, his house in the West Riding, which took its name from a ruined abbey nearby. The rebuilding of Bolton Abbey – in which Robertson probably had a hand – was a most ambitious undertaking. "It will be a big job altogether," wrote Paxton to Sarah from Bolton, "and one that I am sure will do me great credit." He could be perfectly frank with Sarah, without seeming boastful; for she understood how much he wanted to increase his reputation as an architect. "I am already here as at Chatsworth, not a thing can move but I must be consulted and everybody pays court and cringing to me which to tell you the truth rather annoys me."

The Duke, wrote Paxton later, was "wonderfully pleased" with the designs. And, perhaps as a reward, he approved the addition of two glasshouse wings to Barbrook, Paxton's house, one of which could be used as a sitting-room in the summer months.

Towards the end of 1841 Queen Victoria, who had come to the Throne in 1837, paid a visit to Chatsworth with her husband, Prince Albert, the Prince Consort. Privately, the Duke found the Queen gracious but somewhat dull; but he knew what was expected of him and arranged for her to be given a royal welcome. As her carriage entered the park guns fired a salute; and a carefully chosen house party had been assembled in her honour.

Paxton was in his element, for he had been allowed to stage a particularly splendid display of illuminations. The Queen and her husband watched from one of the drawing-room windows; and, at a given signal, all the cascades, waterfalls and fountains burst into shimmering light. The Great Conservatory had been hung with thousands of glowing lamps for the occasion and it looked like some enchanted tropical forest.

During their visit the Queen and the Prince paid a special visit to Barbrook. They examined the books in Paxton's library; and the Queen accepted from Paxton nine volumes of his *Magazine of Botany* and the *Pocket Botanical Dictionary*. She and her husband were very impressed to find that a man who had started life as a gardener's boy was now recognized as a botanical scholar, an architect, engineer and inventor. She had not forgotten how clever he had been in arranging for the gardens to be swept on the occasion of her first visit to Chatsworth. He had been equally efficient this time. On the evening of the illuminations the gardens had been filled with visitors; but an army of labourers worked throughout the night, and by morning everything had returned to normal.

The Duke of Wellington, England's most famous soldier, who was among the guests staying in the house, could scarcely believe his eyes when he got up next morning to find the grounds in perfect order. "I should have liked that man of yours for one of my generals," he remarked to his host. This remark pleased the Duke of Devonshire immensely. "Paxton has outdone himself," he wrote proudly in his diary. "Mr Paxton is quite a genius," wrote the Queen in her journal. She had been particularly impressed by that "mass of glass", the Great Conservatory.

Some time after the Queen's visit Paxton set to work

on a most ambitious engineering feat. The Duke had told him that the Emperor Nicholas I of Russia was coming to England in the early summer of 1844. The Duke was a friend and relative of the Emperor's and had attended his coronation during Paxton's first year at Chatsworth.

"I am expecting the Emperor to visit Chatsworth," said the Duke to Paxton, six months before he was due to arrive, "and I should like something unique to mark the occasion. It must be something he could not see anywhere else, not even at Windsor."

Paxton considered the matter. "What about a fountain, your Grace?" he asked.

"A fountain?" The Duke was scornful. "The Emperor must have seen hundreds of fountains, and he will see dozens more here. You probably don't know it but there is a fountain in the gardens of his palace at Peterhof with a spray which rises to an altitude of 120 feet. The water-works at Perterhof are famous. No, my dear Paxton, you must think again."

"Peterhof is not the highest fountain in the world, your Grace," said Paxton smoothly. "The highest fountain at present is in the State of Hesse-Cassel. Its altitude is 190 feet."

"How do you know that?" the Duke demanded.

"Because," replied Paxton, laughing, "I've been wondering for some time if we couldn't beat that record."

"And could we?" The Duke sounded interested.

"I'm quite sure we could, your Grace. Chatsworth is ideal for the purpose because we have good storage facilities for water as well as an excellent supply. I believe I could build you a fountain which would make the Peterhof fountain look like a dwarf, and the Hesse-Cassel fountain also!" The short, stocky figure of Paxton seemed to grow taller as he spoke.

"What height have you in mind?" asked the Duke curiously.

"At least 260 feet, probably 265 or 267," replied Paxton. "I know I can do it," he went on eagerly, "if only you will say the word."

The Duke could not resist such a challenge. He knew perfectly well that the construction of the fountain would cost a great deal of money; but since Paxton was convinced he could produce this marvel the Duke was not the man to stop him. "Very well," he said generously, "you may do as you please. There's very little time, though. Do you think the fountain will be ready in time for the Emperor's visit?"

"It must be, your Grace," said Paxton fervently; and he hurried off to arrange for a preliminary survey to be made.

The construction of the Emperor Fountain, as the new fountain was to be called, involved a great deal of engineering work. A new water channel had to be made: it was called the Emperor Stream and was $2\frac{1}{2}$ miles long. The stream was on high ground, well above the level of the house, and below it a new lake was constructed. The Emperor Stream supplied the lake with water; and an iron pipe led from the lake to the fountain itself, which was placed in a pond to the south of the house. Paxton himself directed the work, which was pushed ahead as quickly as possible. After weeks of uncertainty the fountain was pronounced ready; and the Duke gave orders that it should play for the first time before the Emperor.

And then the bombshell was dropped. The Emperor informed the Duke that as his visit to England was to be very brief he could not spare the time to travel north to Chatsworth. Instead, the Duke had to go to London to meet him. At the Duke's request, Paxton organized a magnificent banquet at Chiswick House which the Emperor graciously attended. The Duke described to the Emperor the splendours of the fountain he would never see and the part which Paxton had played. In recognition of Paxton's work on the banquet as well as the fountain the Emperor gave him permission to dedicate the next volume of his *Magazine of Botany* to him; and, to Paxton's amazement, created him a Knight of St Vladimir and presented him with a sable coat and three large silver-gilt beakers.

"My dearest and best Nicholas has sent Paxton an order, and a fine present, well deserved," wrote the Duke exultantly in his diary. He knew that in honouring Paxton, his servant, the Emperor was also paying *him* a compliment, as Paxton's master.

If Nicholas I of Russia never saw the Emperor Fountain play hundreds of other people came to see and admire. It had, of course, been very costly to install; and although the Duke's income was very large indeed it was clear that he was overspending. Benjamin Currey, the Duke's lawyer, had long thought that the Duke was too extravagant; and, with his agreement, Paxton now worked out a plan by which, after selling some of his land in Yorkshire and Ireland, the Duke could pay off all his debts and start afresh. It is true that Paxton had encouraged the Duke in his spending; but when the time came he was able to produce with his usual speed and efficiency a plan to set things right.

Of all the schemes which Paxton invented and carried out for the Duke one other became world famous. He had been anxious for some time to grow at Chatsworth a species of giant water-lily, which had been discovered by botanists in Peru in 1801 and in British Guiana in 1837. The water-lily was called *Victoria Regia*. When fully grown *Victoria Regia* had leaves from five to six feet in diameter and a wonderful flower with hundreds of petals shading from rose-pink to white. Seeds of this lily were taken to Kew in 1846 but the plant refused to flower. Three years later Paxton decided to try his luck, and he got permission from the Director of Kew Gardens to take one of the plants to Chatsworth. Everything was in readiness beforehand. Paxton had had a special twelve foot square tank made with a high mound of earth in the centre which would resemble as far as possible the lily's natural home. The tank was placed in one of the greenhouses; and the greenhouse was heated and lit with lamps to imitate natural conditions in the tropics.

On August 3, 1849, Paxton arrived at Kew at six o'clock in the morning to collect his treasure. The plant was very small and had only five leaves, the largest of them only five-and-a-half inches in diameter. He superintended the packing of the plant, carried it to Euston

Station himself, and caught the nine o'clock train for the north.

At Kew, the plant had made no progress; but it settled down at Chatsworth and began to grow. Once started it grew and spread with tremendous speed. The tank was replaced by one double the size; but even so more room was needed. The great question during the months of September and October was whether or not the plant would flower.

Paxton clucked round *Victoria Regia* like an anxious hen with a single chick. He sent a spate of reports to the Duke, who was staying at his Irish home, Lismore.

"If electric light was not so expensive," wrote Paxton in one of his reports, "I should use it for two or three hours morning and evening all winter. The light it produces is exactly like bright daylight, and would make up for the short winter days." He was trying to think of new ways of making his darling plant more comfortable; but he was also very interested in electricity for its own sake. He was convinced that it had an important future; but what he was actually doing – although he did not know it – was to point the way to the present-day use of electric light in battery hen houses and so on.

In 1849 houses were still lit by lamps or gaslight; and electricity must have been very expensive if Paxton hesitated to use it on *Victoria Regia*. She seemed quite happy without it, however, and on November 4 the longed-for event occurred. "Victoria has shown flower!!" wrote Paxton ecstatically to the Duke. "An enormous bud like a poppy head made its appearance yesterday. It looks like a large peach placed in a cup.

No words can describe the grandeur and beauty of the plant."

The Duke was expecting Paxton to join him at Lismore; but, for once, Paxton made a stand. He was, he wrote, in "a terrible stew" about it; but he could not possibly leave *Victoria Regia* at this crowning moment of her life – and his. So he remained at Chatsworth and watched a whole succession of buds burst into glorious flower. "The sight is worth a journey of a thousand miles," he wrote to the Director of Kew Gardens; and he urged him to come and see this wonder for himself.

Important visitors now flocked to see the sight; and *Victoria Regia*'s fame spread far beyond the gardening world. Queen Victoria was extremely interested in her namesake; and Paxton received a summons to Windsor. There he presented the Queen with a fully opened bud and a leaf. "All the world comes to look," declared the Duke, who had returned from Ireland and was fascinated by the beauty and profusion of *Victoria Regia*'s flowers and the enormous strength and floating power of her huge leaves. By the end of November the plant was still in full flower and showed no signs of fading.

"My love," said Paxton to Sarah one morning, "the Duke wants to borrow Annie for an experiment."

Sarah looked suspicious. "An experiment?" she demanded. "And why Annie?"

Seven-year-old Annie was in the parlour with her parents at the time. "What is it, Papa?" she asked eagerly.

Her father chuckled. "I shan't say a word," he said.

64

"His Grace will tell you himself. Come along, my dear."

"It's not dangerous, is it?" Sarah asked.

"Of course not. His Grace would never put a child in any danger."

Sarah was still suspicious, but she did not forbid the child to go.

Paxton held out his hand to the excited Annie. She walked along beside him, looking demure in her full-skirted dress over frilly petticoats and long frilly drawers.

"I'm coming with you," called Sarah. "Just wait till I put on my bonnet and shawl."

Annie hopped about impatiently from one foot to the other. "I do wish Rosa was here to share the fun," she said. Annie and her nine-year-old sister were close friends. They were a lively pair, always up to mischief. Rosa, according to her mother, had been getting so wild and daring that at the age of seven she had been sent away to boarding school; and her reports showed that she was just as daring at school as she had been at home. Annie pined for Rosa. Without her she was lonely and at a loose end, for the rest of the family were so much older. But at least she could tell Rosa about this new adventure when she came home at Christmas.

Sarah was ready in a minute; and they set forth, Paxton still holding Annie by the hand.

"Where are we going, Papa?"

"To the lily house, my dear."

The Duke was waiting for them in the lily house. With him was a friend, Lady Newburgh, who was also to take part in the experiment. "Ah, Paxton," cried the Duke, "so you've brought the little victim!"

"Your Grace!" stammered Sarah, and put an arm round Annie's shoulders. Annie's eyes were popping out of her head, but she was not afraid.

"There's no need to be alarmed, Mrs Paxton," said Lady Newburgh soothingly. "His Grace was joking, of course. Annie will be perfectly safe."

"You can trust me, Mrs Paxton," said the Duke. So saying, he took hold of Annie, swung her up in his arms, lifted her over the edge of *Victoria Regia*'s tank, and stood her gently on one of the giant leaves.

Sarah gasped. Annie stood perfectly still, and the leaf did not even tremble under her weight.

"There, Paxton!" cried the Duke. "I knew we were right. "Annie could stand there for hours without damaging the leaf."

"It would support a much heavier load than Annie," replied Paxton. "I reckon it could carry anything up to 200 pounds in weight without feeling the strain. The underside of the leaf is firmly supported by ribs radiating from the centre," he explained; "and these ribs are linked by flanges at the outer edge which prevent them from buckling under a weight. It's a natural feat of engineering," he added, "and a very impressive one."

The Duke nodded and so did Lady Newburgh. Sarah was still looking a little agitated, and she only relaxed completely when Annie was lifted off the leaf and deposited safely at her side.

The world soon heard the story of Annie Paxton and the leaf. The *Illustrated London News* published a picture of the scene; and *Punch* celebrated it in verse:

On unbent leaf in fairy guise
Reflected in the water,
Beloved, admired by hearts and eyes,
Stands Annie, Paxton's daughter.

Accept a wish, my little maid,
Begotten at the minute,
That scenes so bright may never fade –
You still the fairy in it.

That all your life nor care nor grief
May load the wingèd hours
With weight to bend a lily's leaf,
But all around the flowers.

By the following summer *Victoria Regia* had produced no fewer than 140 leaves and 112 flowers; and plants were being raised from seeds taken from the original plant. Twice already she had outgrown her tank; and now Paxton devised a special Lily House and had it erected near his own house, Barbrook.

The Lily House had a flat ridge-and-furrow roof which was supported by iron cross beams. The cross beams, which also acted as gutters, were set on hollow cast iron columns; and – as in his earlier greenhouses – the iron columns acted as drain pipes as well as supports. Wood was used in the roof and also in the sides of the Lily House, which were made of wood and glass. There was a slatted floor; and the roof was fitted with a clever adjustable contrivance which reinforced the gutters and also made it possible to tilt them to any slope required.

Paxton's design for the Lily House roof was based on the lily leaf, with its flat upper surface and its underside strengthened by a system of ribs. He arranged to heat the greenhouse with pipes running round the inside at basement level, and he ventilated it by openings in the basement walls. For extra ventilation there was a simple device which opened the lights of the roof. The new Lily House contained eight small tanks for water plants; and in the centre there was an immense circular tank. This was equipped with its own heating pipes and cold water supply; and it had four little water wheels which kept the water in gentle motion. As before, *Victoria Regia*'s roots were embedded in a mound of soil; and in conditions as near as possible to her home in the tropics she floated, vast and very beautiful.

The Lily House was the last of Paxton's great works at Chatsworth; and, as a thank offering, the Duke enlarged and rebuilt Barbrook for him.

Paxton remained the Duke's agent and superintended all the work on his estates; and Sarah continued to play her invaluable part. But by this time Paxton had many outside interests and was in great demand as an architect and engineer. For some years he had been extremely interested in the railways, which he realized had a most important part to play in the country's future prosperity. There were still many people who sneered at the idea of trying to link the whole country with a network of railways. Paxton was all in favour of the idea, and so was Sarah, who was a very shrewd business woman. When Paxton decided to invest some money in railway shares she offered him a large part of her own

£5,000, the money her father had given her. Sarah kept a watchful eye on the stock market. She advised Paxton when to buy or sell; and her advice was so sound that Paxton began to make money. He invested some of this money in shares, the rest in property; and by 1850 he was a rich man.

Paxton's early interest in railway development had been encouraged by an older friend, George Stephenson, the great railway inventor, and Stephenson's engineer son Robert. There was nothing Paxton enjoyed more than travelling in trains. In 1845, for example, he proudly reported a railway trip which had kept him in and out of trains for five days and nights on end.

As the years passed his influence on railway development became more and more important. He was always pressing for advances; and, as the railways developed, his opinions carried great weight. "Paxton has the command of every railway influence in England and abroad except the Great Western," wrote his novelist friend Charles Dickens in 1845. "He is in it heart and purse!" In 1848, after three small railway lines had amalgamated to form the Midland Railway, Paxton became a director of the new company and a power on the board.

As ever, Paxton was anxious to help the working classes. One of his schemes was to organize cheap railway travel for working men. Another was to provide suitable work for the unemployed. A third was to reinforce the work of the reformers who were seeking to improve the health of the people by providing better sanitation.

Apart from his many building schemes outside

Chatsworth, Paxton decided in 1845 to break into the newspaper world. He launched a new paper – the *Daily News* – and invested a large sum of money in it. He appointed Dickens as editor, an extremely sound appointment, he thought. Unfortunately, however, everything went wrong. Dickens might be a novelist of genius but he was no good as the editor of a daily paper. He left after three weeks; and he was followed by one editor after another, all of them quite unsuitable. The paper never really got into its stride. In the end Paxton called in an expert, and under the expert's direction things began to improve. Paxton had learned his lesson: newspapers, he concluded, were not in his line. He took no further part in the running of the *Daily News*, which made an excellent recovery and became one of the leading newspapers in the country. As far as Paxton was concerned, it was one of his very rare failures.

Sarah Paxton was thankful to see the end of her husband's association with the paper. She hated him to be away from her, and was sure that he was ruining his health with all the extra work and anxiety. He was frequently away on one or other of his jobs: and her letters to him show how much she longed for his return.

Sometimes Paxton travelled in England, sometimes overseas. In 1846 he spent two months touring Germany and Austria with George Stephenson and two other friends. At Munich the party met the Duke of Devonshire, who was on his way to Italy. The Duke told Paxton that the King of Bavaria, who was in Munich at the time, wished to meet him and George Stephenson. Stephenson, a gentle, unassuming elderly man, was alarmed at the prospect of meeting the King. "Mr Stephenson was in a pretty stew," wrote Paxton to Sarah later, "as he said these great folks did not quite fit in with his previous habits." Stephenson was even more nervous when he heard that although the King could speak English he was very deaf. Paxton was not at all worried. He met the Duke's friends on equal terms: he had spoken with Queen Victoria; and he was not in the least intimidated by kings – even deaf kings. He did most of the talking at the interview, leaving Stephenson to nod and smile. The King was very interested; and he asked Stephenson and Paxton to give him their autographs. He was delighted, he told them, at having met "two such distinguished men".

Everywhere they went the travellers were splendidly entertained, and Paxton returned home well pleased with the trip. Sarah, as always, had looked after Chatsworth in his absence; but she hoped in vain that he would not go away again.

Although Sarah had chosen to remain in the background and longed to keep her husband at home, she did not try and keep her daughters always at her side. The girls were sent to the best schools of the day (they were poor by present-day standards); and every month a box of books arrived from London. The Duke, who was fond of them all, allowed them the run of his house and grounds; and they grew up to love and understand beautiful things.

They were exceedingly proud of their father's growing importance. "I am quite a personage among the other girls," wrote Emily, the eldest, from boarding school, "owing to the fame of my dearest talented father." Emily, who was rather prim, grew up to look something like Queen Victoria – small and round; Blanche was gay and witty; Victoria was studious and serious-minded. George was always the misfit. This, perhaps, was partly because as the only son too much was expected of him. Laura, the fourth daughter, was sweet and gentle. While still at school she was discovered writing letters to a boy; and Sarah was so shocked that she packed the girl off to school in Germany for what she called her "sad disobedience". Rosa and Annie, always the closest of friends, never lost their childish sense of fun.

Sarah kept a strict watch over the older girls; but her ever growing work for Chatsworth and her care for her husband's business interests gave her so much to do that she was less firm with the younger ones. The Paxtons were a united family. Parents and children loved one another dearly; and the children were encouraged to think and speak for themselves. This was unusual in Victorian days, when children were supposed to be seen and not heard; and it made the children both interesting and independent.

When the elder girls grew up they had a gay social time. They went to receptions, balls and concerts and had a number of admirers. Their father was generous with presents, and they were always well dressed. In 1851 Emily, Blanche and Victoria accompanied their father to Lismore and were entertained at a house party by the Duke of Devonshire. Sarah had refused to go; but Paxton wrote home proudly to tell her that the girls were a great success. They enjoyed living a gay life immensely; yet to them, as to their mother, Chatsworth was the most beautiful place in the world, and Barbrook the best possible home.

CHAPTER FIVE

Design for the Crystal Palace

During the late 1840s Prince Albert, the Prince Consort, who was a wise and very intelligent man, began to turn over in his mind the idea of holding a great exhibition of industry in London. As the idea took shape it seemed to him that such an exhibition should show all that was best in British industry and in the industries of the other nations of the world. In this way it would help trade; and, even more important to the Prince, it would be a gesture of peace and universal brotherhood.

The Prince was President of the Society of Arts; and so he invited four members of the Society to meet him at Buckingham Palace in the summer of 1849. He explained his idea and asked if they would be willing to submit it privately to some of the leading manufacturers of the country. If the response was favourable, he said, perhaps they could proceed.

The response was exceedingly favourable. Five thousand influential men banded themselves together to help promote the Prince's idea. A Royal Commission, with the Prince as President, was set up in January, 1850, to put the idea into practice; an executive committee, a finance committee and a building committee of commissioners were formed, and subscriptions and guarantees were collected. A site for the exhibition building was secured on the south side of Hyde Park, covering about twenty-six acres of land.

Although the idea was the Prince's he wished to remain as far as possible in the background. His position in the country was a difficult one: he was not a popular figure; and many people resented his influence over the Queen. It was clear, however, that without his help the scheme might founder; and so he was persuaded to take the lead and to make a number of public speeches expounding his idea and the objects of the exhibition. The exhibition was to be called the Great Exhibition of the Works of Industry of All Nations; and it was to be held during the summer and early autumn of 1851.

There were a number of obvious snags. First of all, since the exhibition was to be an international affair, a vast building would be needed; and the question was, could it possibly be ready in time? If the building was to be constructed of brick – and most people thought that it must be – then an enormous quantity of bricks would be dumped for weeks on end in Hyde Park and would spoil everybody's pleasure. Then, too, there were a number of fine elm trees growing on the site. When tree-loving people learned that some of these trees had already been cut down they banded together and made a strong protest. As a result, the felling was stopped.

In the meantime the Building Committee had troubles of its own. It had invited the citizens of all countries to submit designs for the building. A total of 233 designs had been received: none was suitable. In desperation the Committee set to work to produce a design of its own.

The Committee's design was to be made public before the end of June, 1850. On June 7 Joseph Paxton went to see a friend, John Ellis, MP, the Chairman of the Midland Railway. The two men met in the House of Commons to discuss railway business. A competition for a design to rebuild the Houses of Parliament had been won in 1836 by the architect Charles Barry, who was now a member of the Exhibition Building Committee, and the buildings were nearing completion. Paxton was in the House when the Chamber was tested for sound. It was plain to him that the acoustics would not be good. He had heard rumours that the Building Committee of the Great Exhibition had run into difficulties and guessed that mistakes were being made over the exhibition as they were over the House of Commons. He told Ellis of his fears. "I'm very much afraid," he said, "that a blunder will be made in the building for the Industrial Exhibition."

"Have you seen the Committee's plan, then?"

"I've seen nothing. But from what I hear the thing will be both outrageous and ruinously expensive." Paxton paused to let his words sink in. "I have a notion in my head . . . ," he murmured.

"*You* have a notion?" cried Ellis eagerly. "For Heaven's sake let's hear it!"

Paxton said he must first find out if it was not too late to submit a design; and Ellis, who had the greatest faith in Paxton's abilities, suggested that they should consult Lord Granville, a member of the Finance Committee, at the Board of Trade. Lord Granville was the Duke of

Devonshire's nephew and Paxton knew him well. Ellis and Paxton walked round to the Board of Trade but Lord Granville was not in the building. Instead, they were invited to see Henry Cole, a member of the Exhibition Executive Committee. Cole explained that the specifications of the Building Committee's design were being drawn up, but that he believed it would be possible to insert a clause in the agreement permitting further entries to be made before the final decision was reached.

"Well," said Paxton heartily, "if you will introduce such a clause I will go home and in nine days' time I will bring you my plans, all complete."

Henry Cole looked faintly disapproving. Paxton was merely being boastful, he thought. All the same he promised to do his best to ensure that the clause was introduced.

"You think me a conceited fellow?" asked Paxton who had noticed Cole's disapproving look. "I know my promise must sound more like romance than common sense, but I shall keep it, never fear."

The clause was duly inserted in the agreement; but, apart from Ellis, no one thought there was the remotest possibility that Paxton would be able to keep his word.

Although he was convinced that he knew exactly what was wanted Paxton was unable to get down to the job straight away. June 7 was a Friday. Nothing could be done over the weekend; and on the Monday he had promised to go to Wales to keep an important engagement. This was to see his friend Robert Stephenson float into place the third tube of his great railway bridge over the Menai Strait which separates the Isle of Anglesey from Caernarvon. The bridge – called the Britannia – was constructed to allow trains to pass through an immense rectangular tube of wrought iron; and it was a tremendous engineering feat.

Before he left London for Wales Paxton examined the site in Hyde Park and fixed in his mind the probable size of the building. On Tuesday, June 11, he was in Derby to take the chair at a Midland Railway meeting. The meeting had been called to discuss a minor offence which had been committed by a railway pointsman and to decide what action should be taken.

In front of the Chairman's seat was a large sheet of clean blotting paper; and during the meeting Paxton was seen to make notes on it.

"As you seem to have noted down the whole of the evidence," said one of his fellow directors when the evidence had been heard, "we will take the decision from you."

Paxton smiled. "I know all about the pointsman's case," he answered. "His offence was a very trivial one and I suggest a fine of five shillings."

The other directors agreed. Then Paxton held up the sheet of blotting paper for them to see. "This, gentlemen," he added with a flourish, "is not the evidence but a design for the Great Industrial Exhibition to be held in Hyde Park."

"My dear fellow," gasped one of the directors, "you don't mean to say that you worked it out while we were arguing about the pointsman!"

"Well," replied Paxton, "I won't say that I hadn't

given the matter some thought over the past few days, but I haven't had a moment till now to put anything on paper. Of course it's not finished," he added, "but it won't take long to complete."

The sketch was for a building made of glass and iron based on the lines of the Lily House at Chatsworth.

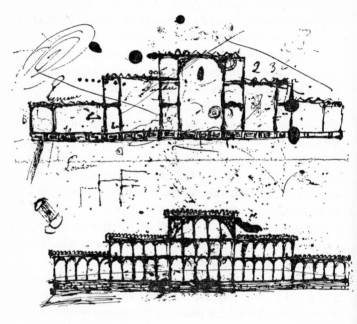

Paxton took the sketch home with him that evening and sat up all night working on the outline for the finished design. For the next eight days he slaved at his drawings. He had the expert help of his staff and also of William Henry Barlow, engineer to the Midland Railway. Barlow gave him some invaluable advice on how to calculate the strength of the columns and girders which would support the building.

On June 21 Paxton took the train for London, carrying the finished plans with him. At Derby station he ran into Robert Stephenson, who was a member of the Building Committee, and the two men got into the train together.

"What luck!" cried Paxton. "We must get a carriage to ourselves, for I have a plan to show you."

"A plan?" asked his friend. "What sort of plan?"

"For the Exhibition building," said Paxton calmly.

"You can't be serious!" exclaimed Stephenson as they settled themselves into an empty carriage. "Besides, you're too late. The whole thing is settled and decided, and our plan will be published in the *Illustrated London News* tomorrow."

Paxton was not perturbed. He reminded Stephenson of the clause which had been inserted in the agreement, a fact which Stephenson had forgotten.

"Have you dined?" he enquired as he opened a hamper of food which he had brought with him from home.

Stephenson replied that he had.

"Then you look at the plans while I eat my dinner."

Stephenson took the plans and began to study them. He was smoking a large cigar; but as the minutes went by Paxton noticed that the cigar had gone out and his friend was far too absorbed in the plans to see what had happened. At length Stephenson looked up. "Admirable!" he cried warmly as he rolled up the plans and handed them back.

Paxton grinned. "You think my design will be accepted?" he asked.

"I only wish it could be. But, as I told you, it's too late, agreement or no agreement."

"But could you at least make sure that the Commissioners see my plans?"

"Of course, my dear fellow, of course; I'll do everything I can. You must see Lord Granville in the morning; and if he agrees the plans can be put before the Commission which meets later in the day."

Stephenson realized that Paxton's plans were far better than the Building Committee's design. The Commissioners examined them but came to no decision. They were awaiting public reaction to their own plans.

On June 22 – the same day – the Building Committee's design was published in the *Illustrated London News*. It was for a brick building four times the length of Westminster Abbey, with an immense dome much larger than the dome of St Paul's. The dome for the brick building had been specially designed by the brilliant engineer Isambard Kingdom Brunel.

As soon as the plans were published there was an outcry against them in Parliament and the newspapers. The design was monstrous, it was ridiculous, people cried, and the cost of the building would be prohibitive. The Prince Consort's enemies seized the opportunity of attacking the whole idea; and, as a result, subscriptions, which had been coming in well, began to dwindle. The Prince, almost in despair, wrote to a friend that he feared the scheme would be shipwrecked.

On June 24 the Prince Consort asked Paxton to come

and see him. The Prince and the Queen remembered the efficient, bustling little man at Chatsworth and had admired the Great Conservatory. The idea of a glass and iron building appealed to the Prince although, as he realized, the use of iron and glass was not entirely new. He was much shaken by the storm created by the Building Committee's design and by the personal attacks on himself. He was all in favour of Paxton's design; but he had reckoned without the Building Committee. After considering Paxton's plans several times, the Committee informed him that their own design would be carried out.

This was too much for Paxton, who had no intention of giving way without a fight. The Committee's design was a monstrosity and would be hideously expensive. Among the rejected designs was one for an iron and glass building with five heavy domes of iron and steel. This design would have cost £300,000 to build; but Paxton, who had absolute faith in his own design, knew that his glass and iron building could be erected far more cheaply. Since the Building Committee refused to reconsider his design he sent it to the *Illustrated London News*. It was published on July 6 together with a full description of the building.

Paxton's design was for a rectangular building made of glass and iron and covering eighteen to twenty acres of ground. It had a flat ridge-and-furrow roof, and a system of guttering similar to the system he had perfected in the Lily House. It had an immensely wide nave, a number of aisles and side avenues, and tiers of galleries high above ground level. The roof and the galleries were supported by hollow iron columns linked at the top by a network of iron girders; and at their base they would rest on horizontally laid drainpipes under the flooring.

This design was clearly much more attractive than the Building Committee's. Paxton's building would be beautiful, spectacular, and perfectly suited to the display of goods. There was such an enthusiastic response from the public that the Building Committee withdrew their objection. Paxton was informed that his design would be reconsidered if he could persuade a firm of building contractors to send in an estimate for the cost of the building by July 10.

This gave him four days' grace. There was very little time; but, as the Duke of Devonshire remarked, "I never knew Mr Paxton resolve to undertake what he did not fully accomplish."

Paxton had already shown his plans to a railway engineer friend, Charles Fox, who was a partner in a firm of contractors, Fox and Henderson. Fox had approved the plans and arranged for Henderson, his partner, and R. L. Chance, a glass manufacturer who had also seen the plans, to set to work at once to prepare a detailed estimate.

Fox and Henderson's works were in Birmingham; and during the next few days everybody worked at a feverish pace. There was an immense amount to do; for detailed drawings had to be prepared, and the cost of the iron, wood and glass had to be calculated exactly. A mistake would have been fatal; and there was no time for the figures to be checked. To make matters more difficult, the Building Committee insisted that the plans should be redrawn so that Paxton's design should be identical in size with their own. Even so, the work was done in time. Fox and Henderson's tender was for £150,000 – less than half the estimated cost of the rejected design for a glass and iron building. If the

materials remained their property, they added, and were returned to them when the Exhibition was over and the building dismantled, the cost would be only £79,800.

Fox and Henderson's tender was submitted to the Commissioners on July 10. Paxton and Fox congratulated one another, believing that all would be well. But they were not yet out of the wood. Several other new designs had been submitted; and one, they learned, would be cheaper to build than their own.

Then followed an anxious few days. Paxton was cheered by the support of Robert Stephenson, whose word carried great weight and who was all in favour of his design. "He sticks to me closer than a brother," Paxton wrote to Sarah, who was eagerly awaiting the decision. As for the Duke, he could hardly stand the suspense.

On July 15 Paxton telegraphed triumphantly to Sarah that his design had been accepted. It had; but there were a number of difficulties still to be overcome. The main trouble was that there were still a good many people who thought the Exhibition should not be held at all. Their spokesman was Colonel Sibthorp, MP, leader of the tree-lovers who had protested against cutting down the elm trees in Hyde Park. Colonel Sibthorp put his case in Parliament. The Government would be guilty of damaging valuable private property in the Park, he declared, if they persisted in their plans for an exhibition building. And all for what? He was absolutely sure that the Exhibition would be a gigantic failure and would make Britain a laughing-stock among foreign nations. Although Colonel Sibthorp had been defeated in the House of Commons he returned to the attack again and again.

"It looks as though the building will have to go up over the Colonel's dead body," remarked Paxton to Fox as they talked the matter over in Fox's office.

"What is he saying now?" asked Fox, a youngish, pleasant looking man with a very intelligent face.

"He says he gathers that the feeling in the country is that the Exhibition is nothing but a fraud and a humbug, and that it will cost at least £240,000."

"What nonsense!" cried Fox. "He knows as well as we do that the job can be done for less than £80,000 if the materials remain our property."

"Of course he knows it, but he prefers not to admit it. He is also saying that it's the people of this country who will have to foot the bill when the time comes."

"But the whole idea, surely, is that the Exhibition will pay for itself. People will flock to it in their thousands, foreigners as well as English people. Just think of all the gate money that will be taken!"

"I should like people to be allowed in free of charge," said Paxton thoughtfully, "poor people at any rate."

"The Government would never allow that," replied Fox. "The Exhibition must pay its way or there'll be real trouble."

"We've trouble enough as it is," said Paxton. "The Colonel has started a 'Committee for the Protection of Hyde Park' in the hope of killing the Exhibition stone dead even at this late hour. *The Times* newspaper is against us too. There's an article in today's issue referring to my monstrous greenhouse. It says that the flat glass roof will leak in every direction and damage the exhibits; that the heat will be overpowering inside the building; and that the cost will certainly be far greater than the estimate." He smiled ruefully. "I'd laugh at all this nonsense if the position weren't still so serious. However," he added more cheerfully, "the *Morning Chronicle* is on our side. It's come out with a strong defence of the Prince Consort's original idea and our right to use Hyde Park. We shall simply have to wait and see and trust that the Government will take a firm line. Britain would certainly be a laughing-stock if the Government allowed the scheme to be scuppered now."

There was one more argument in Parliament before the decision to go ahead was finally taken. Meanwhile, Colonel Sibthorp sent a petition to the Queen begging her to refuse to allow any buildings to be put up in Hyde Park. He had no legal grounds for his argument and the petition came to nothing, much to the relief of the Queen and her husband.

On July 26 the Commissioners assembled to give their official blessing to Paxton's design. His reaction to the good news was to arrange for the church bells in all Chatsworth estate villages to be rung. He and the Duke returned to Chatsworth together to be greeted by a crowd of cheering estate workers and sightseers.

It was indeed a triumph; and if it made Paxton a little vain perhaps he can be forgiven. Everybody was now making a fuss of him; and the Duke was as proud as though the winning design had been his own. "Enchanted with Paxton's work," wrote the Duke in his diary: "the new Lily House, parent of the Great Exhibition." Paxton himself gave the credit to *Victoria Regia*. "Nature was the engineer," he declared in a lecture. "Nature has provided the leaf with longitudinal and transverse girders and supports that I, borrowing from it, have adopted in this building."

Paxton's moment of vanity quickly passed; and his

new success did not change him. "Paxton the quite un-altered gardener," wrote the Duke, who understood him so well. And he was especially pleased when Paxton showed him a letter he had received from the Duke of Wellington. "I knew it would be all right as soon as I heard you had got it," wrote the old soldier.

There were still plenty of problems to be faced. Many people were afraid that a building made chiefly of glass would be dreadfully unsafe; others complained that the heat in summer would be unbearable; and some of the 233 unsuccessful competitors were furious because the prize had been won not by an architect but by a gardener. Then, too, the Building Committee had been made to look foolish. All the same, two of its most distinguished members, Brunel and Barry, now came forward to help Paxton.

One of the chief problems was the clump of elm trees growing on the site. Some of the trees on the site had, of course, already been cut down; but in view of all the protests it was decided that the rest must remain. Somehow or other the trees would have to be embodied in the building. In the end it was decided to cover them with a transept. The transept, which would lie across the main building, would have a curving roof to allow for the height of the trees; and this roof would rise above the flat roof of the main building.

Brunel and Barry helped with the design of the transept. It added greatly to the beauty of the building; and although some people feared that the trees would die they did nothing of the sort, but lived to become a special feature of the Exhibition.

Another objection was now made by the horse riders who used Rotten Row in Hyde Park. The building would get in their way, they complained, and they did not see why a mere exhibition should be allowed to spoil their enjoyment. When the Queen heard of this she was furious. How could they try and ruin the Prince Consort's wonderful idea, she wrote in her journal, "merely for the sake of the Ride in Hyde Park, about which people have suddenly gone quite mad".

The riders could only grumble: they could not take action. And once the decision to build was finally taken the Press had become more friendly. *Punch*, always Paxtons' champion, even made the humorous suggestion that, since Barry was still running into difficulties with the Houses of Parliament, Paxton should be asked to design one glass house for the Lords, another for the Commons.

> Sir, you can do it in a morning. You have only to don your working coat, to clap on your considering cap – that pretty tasteful thing bent from a leaf of the *Victoria Regia* – and the matter is done. Say the word, Mr Paxton: shall the Queen next February open the new Houses of Glass? All we want is your promise. For as the princely Devonshire bears honourable and honouring testimony, Mr Paxton has never attempted anything which he has not succeeded in fully carrying out . . .

Once the problems were settled the main question was whether or not the building with the addition of the transept would be ready by January 1, 1851, when the interior decorators were to take over. Charles Fox promised that it would be ready; and on July 30 his firm took possession of the site and enclosed it in a hoarding.

Surveys now had to be made; calculations of strength had to be worked out; and the girders and ironwork had to be tested. William Cubitt, Chairman of the Building Committee and President of the Institution of Civil Engineers, was appointed by the Commissioners to superintend this work. When the tests and experiments had been carried out he declared that everything was satisfactory and that the building could begin. On September 26 the first of the slender iron columns were fixed in position.

A few weeks later Paxton and Fox stood watching the first iron girders hoisted into place by a team of horses.

"Prince Albert has sent a message to say he would like to have a look round one day next week," said Fox. "Can you be here?"

Paxton pushed the white top hat which he generally wore to the back of his head. "I shall make a point of it," he replied.

"Good! The Prince will want to know precisely what we are going to do – and in great detail. You know his appetite for facts. It'll take the two of us to answer all his questions."

It was a cold wet day in early November when the Prince's carriage drove into Hyde Park. The Prince was escorted into Fox's temporary office, a little building covered in glass and canvas.

"Now, Mr Paxton," said the Prince, who was looking

pale and tired but very dignified and handsome, "I should like to compare your design with the work which is being carried out."

Paxton spread out the plans on the table. "As you see, Sir," he said, "the building will be intersected at the exact centre of the nave by the transept. The roof of the transept will be 108 feet high to cover the elm trees at the northern entrance. There will be eight entrances in all; one at either end of the building and three on each side."

"Quite so," said the Prince. "And the exact height of the main building?"

"It will be 66 feet, Sir. As you know, the building will be made of glass, iron and wood. No stone, plaster or mortar will be used because they would encourage condensation."

The Prince nodded. "And damp would ruin the exhibits," he said.

"Quite so, Sir, and that would never do."

"How many cast-iron columns will you use?" the Prince asked Fox.

"We shall need 3,300, Sir, to support the whole building," answered Fox. "They are being cast into different lengths because we shall want taller columns to support the lower gallery than the upper galleries. The columns will be joined by three-feet sockets which will also support the horizontal girders of the galleries."

"And the columns will be linked at the top by a trellis-work of iron girders," said the Prince. "What special advantage do you expect to get from that?"

It was Paxton's turn to answer. "The girders will be

light but very strong," he said, "and graceful too, we think. And, as you will realize, Sir, the roof will be held up without the need for any interior walls."

The Prince nodded. "And the roof," he said, "the roof, I understand, will be on the ridge-and-furrow principle and made of sheet glass with light wood rafters."

"It will, Sir. The roof of the main building will be flat but it will look rather like a concertina. The ridge-and-furrow rafters will be laid in lines the whole length of the roof and will be supported by cast-iron beams. These beams will have a hollow gutter formed in them to receive the rain water from the wooden furrow – or valley – rafters; and the rain will run down through the hollow columns to the drains."

"And the drainpipes will be out of sight?"

"They will, Sir." Paxton explained that the horizontal drainpipes under the pathways would hold the base of the columns in place and so form the foundation of the building. "The floors of the pathways will be made of trellis-board," he continued in answer to a further question. "They will be half-an-inch apart and will rest on sleeper-joists placed four feet apart. This will make walking pleasant and will be easy to keep clean and dry."

"How much material will go into the building?" asked the Prince.

"We shall use 205 miles of grooved sash-bars, Sir," replied Fox, "and 900,000 feet of glass."

"And how much do you reckon the glass will weigh?"

"About 400 tons, according to our estimate, Sir. We

shall also need about 30 miles of guttering tube. But, thanks to Mr Paxton's sash-bar machine and other modern improvements, everything can be made in standard parts and fitted together on the spot."

"This will make it far less costly, I take it," said the Prince.

"Far less costly," said Fox.

The Prince was very impressed by the economy of this experiment in mass production. He led the way out of the office and through a door in the scaffolding. "The galleries will run the whole length of the building?" he asked, looking upwards to the tips of the columns already in place.

"Yes, Sir," replied Paxton. "They will be divided at intervals by cross-galleries and will be approached by iron staircases. From the galleries people will get a good view of the Exhibition below; and the galleries will also be used for the display of some of the lighter goods – silk, cotton, tapestry work, and so on. And as the roof will be covered in with glass the building can be made both light and airy."

"Are you sure that the building will be properly ventilated and not too bright when the sun strikes the roof?"

"We intend to use a canvas cover over a large area of the roof," Paxton told him, "like the cover on the office you have just left. This will act as a shield and it will also allow the passage of a current of air between the canvas and the glass. In very hot weather cold water can be poured on the canvas to cool the temperature inside the building. We are also working out a system of slatted luffer-boarding to be used on the ground floor and at the top of each tier of galleries. This can be opened and shut by machinery, and it will ventilate the building even when it is full of people."

"You think of everything for this beautiful Crystal Palace," said the Prince. "You see," he added with a smile, "I have been reading *Punch*."

Punch had invented the title of "Crystal Palace" for the Great Exhibition; and it is as the Crystal Palace that it has been known ever since.

Paxton was delighted with the title. "I think, Sir," he said in answer to yet another question, "that there is no end to the use we can make of glass and iron." He had hopes that when in due course the Exhibition was closed the Crystal Palace would be allowed to become a permanent winter garden. And at that very moment he was designing a house entirely covered in glass.

Before he left the building the Prince insisted on seeing everything that was to be seen. He examined the machinery for punching and drilling the ironwork; the sash-bar machine; and a number of other engineering devices. His questions showed an intense interest in machinery and a quick understanding of how it worked. And he was full of praise for the speed with which everything was being made and the building was going up.

As the Prince turned to leave the site a foreman who had been on the watch rang a bell. Immediately two thousand workmen slithered down the scaffolding, ran across the ground, and formed up in a crescent behind his carriage. As the coachman whipped up the horses the men flung their caps into the air and gave the Prince a loud cheer.

CHAPTER SIX

Trials and Setbacks

As soon as the news was spread that the Prince Consort had seen the building site all sorts of people began to clamour for permission to see it for themselves. There were so many applications that the Commissioners decided to try and keep the numbers down by charging five shillings a head for admission. The workmen thought this was an excellent idea; for the money was divided between them. But visitors interrupted the work and annoyed Charles Fox with their endless questions. There was one man who claimed the right to come and go as he pleased. He was the Duke of Devonshire; but, as his nephew Lord Granville remarked, "If any exception is to be made for the Duke of Devonshire it could only be as Paxton & Co." This sort of remark amused the Duke. He was delighted to think that Paxton's name was now so famous.

Despite the five shilling charge the rush of visitors continued. The Commissioners, who had been worrying in case the Exhibition did not draw the expected crowds, now began to think in terms of at least a million foreign visitors as well as countless thousands from England. Instead of worrying that the Exhibition would be a failure, the Commissioners now began to worry for fear that it would be too much of a success. Would the crowds be safe, they wondered? The Duke of Wellington was so alarmed that he suggested that a force of 15,000 policemen would be needed to keep order and prevent visitors from being attacked and robbed.

After a good deal of argument it was decided to keep large bodies of police in reserve in case of trouble. It was also decided to recruit a number of guides from the ranks of retired policemen, soldiers and sailors. The guides would meet the trains arriving at the railway stations. They would then conduct the visitors to lodging houses where they would be well looked after and not over-charged. The railways agreed to play their part. They arranged extra train services and undertook to issue return tickets which would include the price of admission to the Exhibition.

Foreign governments now began to make enquiries about the amount of space which would be available to display their goods. British goods were to take up half the space: the remainder was divided among the other countries, France being allotted the largest share. The Great Exhibition was divided into four main classes – Raw Materials, Machinery, Manufactures, and Sculpture and Fine Arts; and foreign goods were to be allowed into the country free of customs duty. The Commissioners also decided to award medals for outstanding exhibits. One medal was to be awarded by a panel of judges to all the exhibitors whose work reached a very high standard. The other – the Council Medal – was to be awarded only for a really outstanding exhibit.

While these and other questions were being argued the building was going up at a tremendous speed. The timbers and girders were raised into position by teams of horses which galloped in and out of the half-finished structure. Workmen clambered up hundreds of ladders, hauled on pulleys, and crept along the miles of guttering; and high up in the roof the glaziers could be seen swinging in their cradles as they fitted the panes of glass.

There were a number of irritating setbacks and delays and several outstanding problems still to be solved. A most tiresome problem was the presence of a single elm tree, the last of the clump which had been cut down before the tree-lovers' protest. It was a miserable, stunted elm, very different from the stately trees in the transept, but permission to fell it was refused and so it had to remain. Sibthorp's Elm, as the tree was called, stood in a most awkward position at the corner of the nave; and a special gallery had to be constructed around its branches.

As for the Colonel, as late as February, 1851, he was still vainly trying to prevent the Exhibition from being held at all. "Would to God," he declared in the House of Commons, "that a heavy hailstorm or a visitation of lightning would put a stop to the further progress of toe work!" He went on to repeat the charge that the building could not possibly be safe. But, in fact, a strong gale which had sprung up in late November had done no harm beyond scattering a few loose panes of glass and knocking down some scaffolding. In the early part of the new year, however, it almost looked as though Colonel Sibthorp's wishes were coming true. The contractors had just finished the outside of the building when the roof began to leak in the spring rains, and the hollow iron columns were choked with water.

These troubles were tackled and overcome and the building was pronounced watertight. But there was still the question of safety. An engineer, Colonel Reid, who had been placed in charge of the building, took this matter in hand. As a precaution against outbreaks of fire he installed stopcocks and hydrants all over the building and forty-four fire stations equipped with hundreds of buckets. He also engaged a squad of little boys whose job it was to get under the floorboards and sweep away the shavings and other inflammable material which might slip through the slatted floor. Colonel Reid tested the various angles of the roof for wind resistance. And one day when the Queen, the Prince and their children came to inspect the building the royal children were fascinated to see truckloads of cannonballs bowling along the galleries to test their strength.

Another unsolved problem was the question of payment. No charge was to be made to the exhibitors; but the Commissioners, who had borrowed the money to pay for the building from the Bank of England, were determined to repay it from the proceeds of the gate money. They had issued a certain number of season tickets at three guineas each, and had agreed on a scale of charges, ranging from £1 on the two days following the opening down to a shilling on certain days of the week.

When Paxton learned what had been decided he was extremely angry. The question of payment had nothing to do with him but he could not resist interfering. He felt strongly that the public – at any rate the poorer members of the public – should be allowed in free of charge. The Commissioners might get their money by charging for admission during the first fortnight only and then setting aside certain days for people who were prepared to pay to see the Exhibition in peace and quiet. All the other days should be free, he thought; and if the Exhibition did not earn enough money to repay the Bank of England then the Government should be asked to foot the bill.

Although his friends considered it most unwise Paxton wrote an open letter to the Prime Minister and sent it to *The Times*. In it, he begged the Prime Minister to take over the Exhibition on behalf of the public and to open it free of charge. His letter did no good at all. It angered the Government and gave fresh ammunition to the Prince Consort's enemies; and although there were some people who felt that he was probably right his suggestion was never seriously considered. If it had been adopted the Exhibition could only have been a financial failure: instead it was a tremendous financial success.

The opening date of the Great Exhibition had been

fixed for May 1; and long before that date foreign goods had been pouring into the country. There were statues and furniture; priceless objects in gold and silver; costly jewellery; tapestries and carpets; china and pottery; and all kinds of industrial machines and inventions.

The Prince Consort and the Commissioners, who had been anxious in case foreign countries would refuse to exhibit, were greatly relieved. But there was more trouble ahead. The Queen had sent invitations to the opening ceremony to the foreign royal families; and, to her intense annoyance, the King of Prussia forbade his son, the Crown Prince, to accept. He had been told, he said, that there was a grave danger of rioting in London and that the British Government had strongly advised the Queen and the Prince to go out of London.

This was nonsense; and the Prince, generally so calm and courteous, was indignant. "The rumour that the Court has been forced to make up its mind to desert London during the Exhibition," he wrote to the King of Prussia, "is one of those many inventions concocted by the enemies of an artistic and cultural venture and of all progress in civilization, to frighten the public. From the very start they have shown remarkable persistence and ingenuity." The Prince went on to give details of his enemies' ingenuity. "Mathematicians have calculated that the Crystal Palace will blow down in the first strong gale, Engineers that the galleries would crash in and destroy the visitors; Political Economists have prophesied a scarcity of food in London owing to the vast concourse of people; Doctors that owing to so many races coming into contact with each other the Black Death of the Middle Ages would make its appearance as it did after the Crusades." Finally, he added, theologians had argued "that this second Tower of Babel would draw upon it the vengeance of an offended God".

The Prince ended his letter on a note of sarcasm. "I can give no guarantee against these perils," he wrote, "nor am I in a position to assume responsibility for the possibly menaced lives of your Royal relatives. But I can promise that the protection from which Victoria and I benefit will be extended to their persons – for I presume we also are on the list of victims."

When he received the Prince's letter the King of Prussia was shamed into giving the Crown Prince and his family permission to go to England. All the same, the British Government was uneasy. There were rumours that dangerous foreign revolutionaries were planning to enter the country disguised as ordinary visitors; that they would stir up a revolt and proclaim a republic. Amidst all the turmoil the Prince and the Queen remained resolute and calm. The Queen had made up her mind to open the Exhibition in public, at a ceremony attended by royalty and distinguished people from all countries as well as by the season ticket holders. She was exceedingly angry when, almost at the last minute, the Commissioners lost their nerve; and the Prime Minister, who feared for her safety, advised her to open the Exhibition at a private ceremony.

The Queen was no coward. She was certain that there was not the slightest danger of a revolution and she did not fear assassination. Her people loved her, she knew, and she felt that she and her husband would be perfectly safe in their midst. Besides, apart from anything else, she had no intention of spoiling the pleasure of the 8,000 season ticket holders, many of whom were coming to London especially to see their Queen.

Queen Victoria got her way. On April 20, less than a fortnight before the opening, it was announced that the ceremony would be held in public.

Details of the ceremonial now had to be worked out in a great hurry. And right to the last minute finishing touches were still being made to the building. While the exhibitors unpacked and arranged their goods the interior decorators were painting the ironwork in shades of blue, red and yellow and decorating the 3,300 slender iron columns with yellow stripes. The columns had been continued through the roof as flagstaffs; and each was to fly the flag of one or other of the nations exhibiting.

As the last days of April went by statues were being hauled into place and draperies were being hung. The tiers of seats for the spectators were being hurriedly put together; and it was now known that there would be 12,000 spectators instead of the original 8,000. The sound of hammering filled the vast building and mingled with the hiss of steam escaping from the funnels of the steam engines in Britain's machinery section.

Few people believed that the Great Exhibition could be ready in time. The visitors who thronged Hyde Park could see the final touches being made to the paintwork on the outside of the building. At ground level the building was protected by boarding; and each storey was decorated with an iron cornice and crest. Above the north entrance rose the glimmering glass roof of the transept, adding greatly to the beauty of the building. The people were entranced. The Crystal Palace was a gorgeous building, far more splendid than they had imagined; and the British among them swelled with pride.

Not so Colonel Sibthorp. He made one last effort to sabotage the whole affair and declared in public that his dearest wish was that "that confounded building called the Crystal Palace might be dashed to pieces". The Colonel was delighted with the rumour that the elm trees in the transept were infested with sparrows which had begun to ruin the valuable exhibits. The Commissioners were apparently unable to cope with the menace; and the Queen was believed to have sent for the Duke of Wellington, who was Ranger of Hyde Park. "Try sparrow hawks, Ma'am," was the Duke's advice.

This rumour may or may not have been true: but the elms were in splendid leaf by the opening day and there was not a sign of any sparrows.

Two days before the opening the Queen inspected the Crystal Palace. She spent several hours in the building and insisted on seeing everything; and poor Charles Fox, who was frantically busy making sure that everything was in order, had to escort her and answer all her questions. That evening the Queen wrote an impression of the scene in her journal. She was, she declared, "quite beaten, and my head bewildered, from the myriads of beautiful and wonderful things which now quite dazzles one's eyes! Such efforts have been made, and our people have shown such taste in their manufactures! All owing to this great Exhibition and to Albert – *all to him!* We went up into the gallery, and the sight from there, with the numerous courts full of all sorts of objects of art, manufactures, etc., is quite marvellous. The noise was overpowering, for so much was going on everywhere, and from twelve to twenty thousand people engaged in arranging all sorts of things."

The Queen had no doubt at all that the opening would go smoothly. Her husband was far from certain. "Terrible trouble with arrangements for the opening," he wrote gloomily in *his* diary.

On April 30 Charles Fox was called away from his work again to conduct the Queen, Prince Albert and the Crown Prince and Princess of Prussia round the building. The scene was as busy and noisy as before; but by this time tall palm trees, plants, and pots of growing flowers were being moved into place, and fountains were beginning to play. The Queen was tremendously excited; and the Prince was less gloomy than before. Charles Fox was thankful when the royal visitors had departed. Now at last he was free to complete his job.

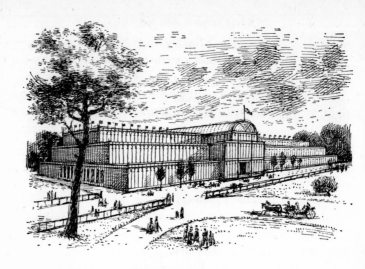

CHAPTER SEVEN

Grand Opening

May Day had been declared a public holiday; and the exhibitors were still giving their goods a final brush-up when the first visitors arrived in Hyde Park soon after eight in the morning.

The whole Paxton family was in London for the event. Sarah and the girls had new bonnets and gowns, and Paxton wore Court dress with a cocked hat. He was growing very portly and stout; but the girls agreed that nobody, not even the Prince, would look better. Sarah and the family were to watch the proceedings from seats in the front row of one of the galleries. Paxton was to join the Duke of Devonshire on the ground floor.

The morning was bright, though still a little cool, when the Paxtons' hired carriage drove into Hyde Park. They entered the building by the north entrance; and the moment he set foot inside the transept Paxton felt that all was well. The elm trees towering towards the curved roof were a spectacle in themselves; there were plants and flowers everywhere; and in the very centre of the transept a huge crystal fountain flung its gleaming jets of water high into the air. Statues were grouped about the fountain. There were huge figures on horse-back; heroes and heroines from the Bible, from history, and from Greek and Roman legends; and they all looked very white against a background of bright red hangings. The royal dais faced the fountain. It had been placed under a gold embroidered canopy, and it was covered by a carpet which had been worked in wool for the Queen by one hundred and fifty loyal ladies. More groups of statues stood beyond the dais; and to the east and west of the fountain stretched the nave and aisles of the main building, with the galleries above. The building was full of exhibits, yet the general effect was one of space, air and light; and Paxton was thankful to see that the canvas awning over the transparent roof would provide shelter from the rays of the sun.

Part of the ground floor of the building had been cordoned off for spectators; other spectators were be-ginning to climb up to the galleries. They had a long time to wait before the Queen's arrival; but meanwhile they could watch the arrival of diplomats, Officers of State, ministers and foreign ambassadors, some of them dressed in the colourful clothes of their office. There was

a special cheer for the Duke of Wellington, for this was his eighty-second birthday; and there were murmurs of approval for the Gentlemen-at-Arms in their golden helmets and foaming white plumes; the Yeomen of the Guard and the heralds who were to guard the ceremonial iron gates; and the State trumpeters in their gold coats and black velvet caps.

The streets between Buckingham Palace and Hyde Park were densely lined with people. At twenty minutes to twelve the royal party of nine carriages left the Palace with an escort of the Household Cavalry. For a few moments it looked like rain; but the clouds passed and the sun appeared. The crowds cheered; and their cheers became a roar as the last carriage appeared. In it were the Queen, Prince Albert, and their two eldest children, the Princess Royal and the Prince of Wales.

The carriages entered Rotten Row just before noon. The arrival of the Queen was heralded by a fanfare of trumpets. As she entered the Great Exhibition building the Royal Standard was hoisted on the transept roof, and the Yeomen of the Guard opened the ceremonial gates.

The Queen, who was wearing a dress of pink and silver brocade with the ribbon and armlet of the Garter, looked as young and excited as a girl. She held the hand of the ten-year-old Prince of Wales, who was wearing a kilt. Behind her walked Prince Albert, hand-in-hand with the Princess Royal, who was dressed in white satin with a wreath of wild roses in her hair. When the royal family passed into the transept they were greeted by cheers and rounds of applause. As the Queen stepped on to the dais the National Anthem was sung by the massed choirs of Westminster Abbey, St Paul's Cathedral, St George's Chapel, Windsor, and the Chapel Royal, led by world famous professional singers, to the accompaniment of organs and military bands.

When the last notes of "God Save the Queen" had died away the Prince Consort, as President of the Royal Commission, stepped down from the dais to stand at the head of the waiting Commissioners. He then read aloud the Commission's report on the Great Exhibition which contained a mention of the debt which the Commissioners owed to Mr Paxton, the architect of the great building. The report ended with the prayer that the Great Exhibition, which had as its aim "the promotion of all branches of human industry, and the strengthening of the bonds of peace and friendship among all nations of the earth", would "be long remembered among the brightest circumstances" of Queen Victoria's reign.

Smiling happily, the Queen read a short reply in her clear, bell-like voice. Then the Archbishop of Canterbury recited a solemn prayer and a blessing; and, after a hushed pause, the massed choirs burst into the strains of the *Hallelujah Chorus* from Handel's *Messiah*. During the singing the Royal Procession moved into place for a tour of the building.

At this solemn moment there was a stir among the officials surrounding the dais. A number of people had noticed a dignified Chinese clad in satin robes who had been waiting with distinguished officials for the Queen's arrival. Nobody recognized him and, as China had sent no official representative to the opening, they wondered who he could be. When, however, he was seen shaking hands with the Duke of Wellington they were convinced that he was someone important. They did not realize that the Duke had not the slightest idea who he was.

During the singing of the *Hallelujah Chorus*, while the procession was getting into line, the mysterious Chinese pushed his way up to the dais, prostrated himself, and bowed his head to the ground before the Queen. Behaviour of this kind was not on the programme; and several officials stepped hurriedly forward to remove him. But the Queen was more than equal to the occasion. Trying hard not to laugh, she waved the officials aside, and in the most tactful way gave orders that the Chinese should walk in the procession next to the Duke of Wellington. It was not until afterwards that the man's identity was discovered. He was very far from being distinguished. His name was He-Sing. He was the owner of a Chinese junk which was moored at the Temple pier; and he showed visitors over the junk for a fee of a shilling a head. After the opening of the Great Exhibition, when He-Sing could claim that he had walked in the Royal Procession beside the famous Duke of Wellington, his profits went up enormously and he had a record season. Nobody seems to have grudged him his moment of triumph, undeserved though it was.

This was also Joseph Paxton's moment of triumph, the proudest moment of his whole life. At the Prince Consort's special wish he had been chosen to lead the procession. First came the four Pursuivants of Arms;

then came Paxton, with Fox on his right hand, Henderson on his left. They were followed by the Commissioners, British and foreign officials, the heads of Government Departments and the Great Officers of State. Then came the Prince Consort, the inspiration of the Exhibition, looking modestly pleased, with the Queen and their two children; and behind them walked other members of the British and foreign royal families. It was an imposing procession; and so long that it took nearly an hour to tour the transept and the two main aisles and there was no time to inspect the rest of the building.

Among the most impressive exhibits which had been examined were a lace-weaving machine; a patent envelope machine which cut, folded, gummed, and delivered thousands of envelopes an hour and could be worked by a couple of boys; a large-scale model of the Liverpool Docks; and the Koh-i-Noor Diamond, which had recently been presented to the Queen and was displayed in a gilded cage.

The Queen and the Prince had seen almost everything before; and they were to see it all again many times. The opening ceremony, wrote the Queen in her journal that evening, was "a complete and beautiful triumph – a glorious and touching spirit, one which I shall ever be proud of for my beloved Albert and my country. Yes! it is a day which makes my heart swell with pride and glory and thankfulness!" After describing the various happenings the Queen ended with a word of praise for the organizers. "All the Commissioners, the Executive Committee, etc., who worked so hard and to whom such immense praise is due, seemed truly happy, and no one more so than Paxton, who may be justly proud; he rose from being a common gar-ener's boy."

The crowds which thronged the Great Exhibition after the opening day found much to interest them. The Koh-i-Noor was one of the main attractions. So, too, were the statues; the steam engines; the printing machines; and an electric clock which had been fitted into the building over the south entrance. The Medieval Court was considered extremely beautiful, with its stained glass windows, Gothic crosses and altar-pieces, and show-cases of church vestments. For the housewife there was a brand new cooking range, which used gas instead of coal: it was divided into three compartments, and was not very different from the gas cookers of today. Everybody wanted to see the Prince Consort's Model Lodging House. This had been designed to house several working-class families, each in a separate suite of rooms; and it was really the origin of our modern blocks of flats. Although some of the exhibits from foreign countries – especially those from France – were considered more beautiful and artistic than the British, the quality of British workmanship, particularly in machinery, was far and away the best; and Britain was well ahead of her rivals in industry and manufacture.

The finest and most popular exhibit of all was the Crystal Palace itself. The crowds were fascinated by the vast glass building which glittered in the sunshine like a fairy tale palace. Those who knew something about design and decoration could see that it was ideally suited to its purpose. The flat glass roof of the main building, the soaring roof of the transept, the slender iron columns, seemed exquisitely light and lovely to people who were used to heaviness and gloom in architecture. Almost everybody agreed that the building could not have been better. It was, in fact, very much over-praised by a few of its most ardent admirers, who compared it with the magnificent buildings of ancient years and claimed that Paxton was one of the greatest architects of all time.

This was a ridiculous claim, and one which Paxton would never have made for himself. He was first and foremost a gardener; but he had a very decided gift for engineering and building, and a mind which was always teeming with original ideas. Naturally, he was proud that his Crystal Palace should be highly praised; and proud, too, to know that the success of the Exhibition had turned the Prince Consort into a national hero. Queen Victoria visited the Great Exhibition privately nearly every day; and her own popularity increased when she talked informally with workmen, exhibitors and visitors.

It was the Crystal Palace which made London so exciting during the spring and summer of 1851. London was full of visitors. The Queen and the Prince entertained their foreign guests at balls and receptions at Buckingham Palace; and the Royal Society and other learned bodies gave receptions for distinguished foreigners. A special event was a dinner of roast beef and plum pudding given by the chief British workmen employed at the Crystal Palace to the foreign workmen.

The climax of the London season was a banquet and

ball held at Guildhall. As the Queen drove from Buckingham Palace to the City she was greeted the whole way by crowds of cheering people. She was overjoyed to think that her adored husband was responsible for this immense success. "Albert's dearest name is immortalized with this great conception, his own," she wrote in her journal. And in a letter to the Prime Minister she wrote that "the Queen . . . feels so proud of being his wife that she cannot refrain from herself paying a tribute to his noble character".

The British functions passed off without a hitch; but when the French decided to repay hospitality it was quite another matter. The city of Paris invited the Prince Consort, the Commissioners and others responsible for the Great Exhibition, and the Lord Mayor and Corporation of London to spend a few days in Paris. The Prince was unable to accept the invitation, but the Lord Mayor accepted on behalf of himself and the Corporation. On August 1 a party of a thousand left London for Paris, Joseph Paxton among them.

The French had generously offered to pay all the expenses; but from the start everything went wrong. After a very rough Channel crossing the visitors arrived in Paris late at night to find that most of them had nowhere to stay and had to spend the rest of the night in station waiting-rooms. To make matters worse a great deal of luggage had vanished, including the robes and regalia of the Lord Mayor and his suite. Distinguished British visitors had to make their first public appearance at a banquet held in their honour dressed in badly-fitting, ready-made clothes which had been hastily bought during the morning. The French did everything they could to put matters right. Rooms were found for the entire party; the luggage was retrieved; and the visitors were entertained at a number of functions, including a gala performance at the opera. All the same, the British found it hard to forgive their hosts for the muddle; and they arrived back in England to be jeered at in the newspapers for having represented their country so poorly.

Paxton had not stayed for all the festivities. He returned to England in time to attend a dinner given in his honour at Derby on August 5. Had he been in charge of the Paris arrangements it is most unlikely that anything would have gone wrong.

Although the Great Exhibition was so popular there was a good deal of ill-feeling about the way the exhibition medals were distributed, and the panels of judges were severely criticized. But every one approved of the major awards. The Great Council Medal was given to the Prince Consort for his work for the Exhibition and his model dwelling-house; to the building contractors Fox and Henderson; and to Joseph Paxton for his design of the Crystal Palace.

The Exhibition was open to the public from May 1 to October 11. October 7 was the most crowded day of all, with nearly 110,000 visitors. Among the visitors was the Duke of Wellington, who had grown very fond of the Exhibition. The old hero had been advised not to go among such a mass of people, but he would not heed the warning. As he stumped up the nave he was recognized and mobbed by a noisy, cheering crowd. The uproar was heard all over the building; and people were afraid that something had gone very wrong and the Crystal Palace was about to collapse. An alarm bell was sounded, and there was a panic rush for the exits. In the excitement a large stand of priceless French china was overturned with a resounding crash. Nobody was hurt; and the broken china was the only accident which occurred during the five-and-a-half months the Crystal Palace had been open. Meanwhile, the Duke of Wellington, looking pale and angry, had been escorted out of the building by six police constables who had been following him at a distance all the time.

On October 11, the final day, the public refused to leave. "God Save the Queen" was played on the organs, but still they would not go. They stayed on, cheering and flinging their hats into the air; and some people wept to think that the Great Exhibition had come to an end. The warning bell was sounded, but still they stayed; and it was late before the building was finally cleared.

The Queen paid her last visit to the Crystal Palace on October 14. "How sad and strange," she wrote in her journal that evening, "to think this great and bright time has passed away like a dream, after all its triumph and success." Next day, without any of the pomp of the opening day, the Prince Consort declared the Exhibition closed.

Joseph Paxton and Charles Fox were knighted for their services to the exhibition. Many people felt, however, that Paxton had earned a higher honour, as the architect of their lovely Crystal Palace. It was quite true that the building, with the various alterations and additions which had been made to it, had cost far more than Fox and Henderson's original estimate. But the attendances had been very much higher than any one had guessed. In all, 6,039,195 people had visited the Exhibition; and their gate money had more than paid all the expenses. When the final figures were counted the Commissioners found themselves with a surplus of £170,000.

Punch, always Paxton's champion, suggested that he ought to benefit from this unexpected windfall. "The Chancellor of the Exchequer is a smiling debtor to Joseph Paxton," wrote *Punch*. "What then for the architect? Mere knighthood? Court gingerbread with no gilding? This will never do. Some small percentage from that quarter of a million is as much the due of Joseph Paxton as was his day's wages to any glazier who worked at the fabric."

A cartoon emphasized *Punch*'s remarks. Called *Praise and Pudding*, it showed the Prince Consort handing Paxton a slice of pudding labelled £20,000.

The Commissioners evidently agreed that Paxton deserved some of the profits, and they gave him £5,000. This was not a large sum; but Paxton was in no need of money. He was a rich man; and, to him, recognition meant much more than money. What he longed for was to keep the Crystal Palace in being. Yet, now that the Exhibition was closed, the empty building was taking up a great deal of valuable space in Hyde Park, and few even of its admirers thought it should be allowed to remain. The question was debated in the House of

Commons on April 30, 1852; and to the unconcealed joy of Colonel Sibthorp, who had never once set foot inside the building, it was decided that the Crystal Palace must go.

In 1852 it was impossible to estimate the exact achievements of the Great Exhibition, apart from its profits. Looking back, it is clear that it certainly did not fulfil the Prince Consort's desire for the brotherhood of man: the nations were just as quarrelsome after the Exhibition as they had been before. The Exhibition had shown the important part which industry was beginning to play in the world and the superior quality of British-made goods: but industry was on the up-grade, and would have forged ahead if the Exhibition had never been held. A great deal was talked and written at the time about the artistic beauty of many of the exhibits: yet most people who have seen relics of the Exhibition or looked at a copy of the enormous illustrated catalogue will probably think them extremely ugly and lacking in artistic merit.

But the Crystal Palace had two undoubted triumphs. First, it provided ordinary working people whose days were dull and drab with a glorious palace of light and glass; and it gave them a taste for amusement combined with instruction.

The second triumph was a real and lasting achievement. The Prince Consort suggested that the surplus money should be spent on the spread of education, especially industrial education. This was a splendid idea. Between them, the Prince and the Commissioners worked out a scheme to create a centre for the learned, artistic and educational societies of the country on a site as near as possible to Hyde Park. An estate of 87 acres was bought in South Kensington, adjoining the Park. Among the buildings standing on the site today are the Victoria and Albert Museum, the Natural History and Science Museums, the Royal Colleges of Art and Music, the Albert Hall, and the Imperial College of Science and Technology.

So the Crystal Palace has its own memorial. Nearby, in Hyde Park itself, stands the Albert Memorial, the nation's tribute to the creator of the Great Exhibition, the Prince Consort, who died in 1861, just ten years after his dream was realized.

CHAPTER EIGHT

The Crystal Palace at Sydenham

The Great Exhibition was dead. "Crystal Palace condemned yesterday by House of Commons," wrote the Duke of Devonshire in his diary on May 1, 1852, the anniversary of the opening day, "so it comes down."

No one knew better than the Duke that the decision would be a bitter blow to Sir Joseph Paxton; but the Duke also knew that Paxton was not only a good fighter but a good loser.

"You're in excellent spirits today," said the Duke when Paxton joined him at Devonshire House the following morning. The Duke was eating breakfast, but Paxton had been up since early morning.

"It's no use crying over spilt milk, your Grace," replied Paxton briskly. "I've taken a hard knock, I won't deny it, but I'm not down yet. The fact is," he added with a grin, "I've got another plan up my sleeve."

"And what may that be?"

"I've had it in mind for some time to move the Crystal Palace to another site, somewhere large and empty. I've got my eye on the very spot in Penge Park in Sydenham. Land's much cheaper in Sydenham than in London."

The Duke nodded. "Even so," he said, "you would need a great deal of money."

"That is no problem, your Grace," said Paxton gleefully. "I've found the money already."

"What? Already?"

"Yes, indeed, your Grace. I have secured a capital of half a million pounds to float a company and finance the scheme. All that needs to be done now is to buy the site and arrange to remove the building."

The Duke laughed. "Just another of those ingenious Paxton schemes?" he exclaimed.

"Just another scheme," said Paxton in a matter-of-fact voice. But, as the Duke well knew, while Paxton had a great many schemes on hand, none was half as dear to him as the future of the Crystal Palace.

Paxton could not, of course, put his other schemes aside and give all his attention to the Crystal Palace. During the spring and summer of 1852 the Duke was often seriously ill and Paxton seldom left his side. However busy he might be, the Duke must always come first: Paxton might now be a famous man but he still looked on the Duke as his master. He could well have afforded to break away and set up on his own; but this he would never do as long as the Duke had need of him.

At this time Paxton was at work on plans to rebuild the Duke's Irish home, Lismore Castle. He was also, on the Duke's behalf, working on plans for the redevelopment of Buxton in Derbyshire, where the Duke owned a great deal of land. At the Duke's request Paxton designed an elaborate layout for the Buxton park. He was at his best designing gardens and parks and he designed a large number.

Two other well known parks which he planned during the 1840s and 1850s were Princes Park in Liverpool and Birkenhead Park opposite Liverpool on the other side of the River Mersey. It pleased him to know that people who lived cooped up in towns and cities could enjoy the space, fresh air, and the trees and flowers of public parks. He was particularly glad, therefore, to be invited to design a twelve-acre People's Park at Halifax in Yorkshire. The People's Park was presented by a rich local manufacturer, Sir Francis Crossley, MP, to the people of Halifax on condition that they looked after it and kept it in order.

For some time now Paxton had been busy with a gigantic house-building project. His influence in the railway and business worlds had brought him to the notice of the great financial wizards of the day, the Rothschild family. In the autumn of 1850 Baron Mayer de Rothschild had asked him to build him a vast country house at Mentmore in Buckinghamshire. Paxton had worked on the designs for Mentmore and the Crystal Palace at the same time. The design for Mentmore was adapted from a sixteenth century house, Wollaton Hall near Nottingham; but it had special features of its own, among them a central court roofed over with glass. Paxton also designed a magnificent park which gave the mansion a perfect setting.

Mentmore was scarcely finished when Paxton started work on Ferrières. This was a mansion not far from Paris which Baron James de Rothschild, a member of the French branch of the family, had commissioned him to build. Later on, Paxton built a house for Baron Alphonse de Rothschild at Geneva; and designed the gardens for another Rothschild house in Paris. He now had the skilled help of a new qualified architectural assistant, George Henry Stokes, who carried out some of the work for him. But Paxton remained the guiding spirit of all these schemes.

The Rothschilds became Paxton's friends as well as his employers, and he was very happy to work for them. The Rothschild houses formed only a fraction – but a very important fraction – of his building schemes. He was in constant demand to design houses and churches, hospitals and public buildings as well as parks and gardens. It is difficult to believe that even with the help of his trained assistants any man could possibly have accomplished so much. But Paxton had an immense appetite for work and tremendous powers of concentration, as well as a mind teeming with new ideas. He was fascinated with every one of his schemes; but the Crystal Palace remained his favourite.

Penge Park, the new site for the Crystal Palace, was on the summit of a hill overlooking Sydenham. To the south and east there was a wonderful view over unspoilt country; to the north and west the hill looked towards London. The site was perfect; and Paxton was convinced that his Crystal Palace, glimmering on the hilltop, would look even more splendid than it had looked in Hyde Park. It was not to be exactly the same. Paxton himself was to be responsible for the new designs and would plan and take charge of the grounds. The old building was bought by the company he had launched; and Fox and Henderson undertook to put up the new one.

The Sydenham Crystal Palace covered a smaller area of ground than the original. It was, however, taller and more magnificent; and the area of glass surfaces was

almost double. The Sydenham Palace had three transepts instead of one, all with curving roofs; and the roof of the nave was arched instead of flat. The nave was planted with trees, shrubs and plants of all kinds, and some of the trees were brought specially from France. The rest of the building was divided into courts, each court representing some aspect of the great art and architecture of the past. In the Egyptian Court, for example, there were models of sphinxes and obelisks and of the colossal seated statues of Abu Simbel. The Grecian Court represented a temple of Jupiter during the fifth century B.C. In the central transept there was an organ and space for an orchestra; and for many years to come the Crystal Palace drew crowds of music lovers to Sydenham.

As the building stood on top of a hill the grounds had to be laid out in a series of terraces. Brunel designed two high water towers which were a feature of the Crystal Palace. They were necessary for Paxton who wanted a plentiful supply of water for his water-works – fountains, cascades and water-temples. The water-temples, which were constructed of glass and iron, were 70 feet high, and each sheltered a group of statues. An elaborate device in the dome of each water-temple controlled a sheet of water which covered the statues with a fine transparent veil and was considered very artistic. There were formal flower gardens on the upper terraces; lower down, a lake, pathways, trees and shrubs formed a pleasant park. Statues representing the Arts and Science were dotted about the grounds; but the exhibit which drew the densest crowds represented Geology. It was a collection of gigantic plaster casts of the prehistoric animals which had once haunted the weald of Sussex and Kent. There were models of the Pterodactyl, the Plesiosaurus and the Iguanodon; and to complete the fantastic illusion, the specimens were grouped together in lifelike attitudes, each species on a separate island.

The Sydenham Palace was not built with the speed of the original. The first iron columns were raised in August, 1852; but when the Palace was opened by the

Queen on June 10, 1854, it was still only half finished
and the water-works had not yet been installed. The
opening ceremony was impressive but it was not such a
brilliant occasion as the opening of the Hyde Park
Palace. But the sun shone, and the Queen, who was
accompanied by the Prince Consort, was full of admiration. A choir of 1,500 sang the *Hallelujah Chorus* to the
accompaniment of a band of 200 brass instruments. A
famous singer, Clara Novello, sang parts of the
National Anthem as a solo. Her high B flat was so
powerful and ringing that it left the audience gasping
with amazement; and the policemen on duty – against
all the rules of discipline – removed their hats in silent
tribute!

The Duke of Devonshire thought the new Crystal
Palace was absolutely perfect. To mark the occasion
he presented Paxton with an inscribed piece of heavy
silver plate, and Sarah with a magnificent bracelet
inscribed with the words "beloved and worthy". In a
letter of thanks, Sarah wrote of the Duke's "unbounded
generosity". The bracelet, "for beauty and elegance sur-
passes anything of the kind I have ever seen". And she
added her husband's thanks for "the grand piece of
Plate . . . with an inscription on it that will cheer our
hearts whilst life is spared to us".

The Duke was a constant visitor to the Crystal Palace.
So, too, was the Queen. In April, 1855, she drove to
Sydenham in state with the Emperor Napoleon III of
France and his lovely Empress Eugénie. The building
was crowded with sightseers; and the Emperor was
nervous at the prospect of walking about among so

many people. But the Queen, who felt entirely safe in the midst of her subjects, reassured him, and the tour of the building passed off without a hitch.

Paxton had prepared a surprise for the royal visitors: the newly installed water-works were to be turned on for the first time in their honour. To his horror the fountains refused to gush. He was almost in despair; and the royal party was getting ready to depart when the technical difficulty was overcome and the fountains flung their glittering spray into the air.

When the Queen visited the Crystal Palace in June of the following year she was greeted by a display of the water-works in all their glory. She drove with her attendants through the grounds in a procession of carriages. Sir Joseph Paxton rode beside the Queen's carriage mounted on a small brown charger. He wore his usual white top hat and one of his favourite brocade waistcoats; and as he had grown extremely portly he looked almost as large as his mount.

The Queen was charmed with the shimmering effect of the water-temples. She also showed the greatest interest in the fantastic collection of prehistoric monsters, which had recently been moved from the grounds to the inside of the building.

"The other evening, Ma'am," Paxton informed the Queen in answer to a question, "a dinner-party of twenty-one people was held inside the body of this monster here."

The Queen was very surprised. "It seems scarcely possible," she exclaimed. "I trust the dinner was successful."

"It was indeed, Ma'am, especially the after-dinner address. A learned professor standing right inside this extinct animal's skull gave the assembled company a lecture on the work of our geologists."

The Queen was deeply impressed, but she had to hide a smile. As she wrote that evening in her journal, "good Sir Joseph Paxton", who had never quite mastered his pronunciation, had shown her the new exhibition room for what he called his "hextinct hanimals!"

The Sydenham Crystal Palace had been designed both to amuse and to educate. It certainly gave pleasure to thousands of people and also added something to their knowledge. But right from the start it was a worry and a burden, especially to Paxton. A fortune had been spent on the Palace and the grounds, and the water-works had been particularly expensive to install. Even so, the supply of water never seemed enough for the constant demand; and despite its popularity the Crystal Palace never managed to pay its way.

It made a big difference in Paxton's life. In order to be on the spot as often as possible he bought Rockhills, a large and comfortable house nearby. Paxton was very fond of Rockhills, which adjoined the grounds of the Crystal Palace. It had a glass-roofed open-fronted veranda with trellis-work which he found ideal for the growing of climbing plants. A flight of stone steps led down from the house to a terrace with raised flower beds filled with blue hydrangeas. The lawn in front of the house was broken up into a number of flower beds; and the kitchen garden was filled with all kinds of fruit and vegetables, some grown under glass in an invention of Paxton's known as "Portable Glass Houses for the Million". The Crystal Palace could be seen from the terrace; but the boundary line between the two properties was hidden by a hedge of gorse and broom.

Rockhills now became Paxton's principal home. He entertained his friends there – businessmen, writers and politicians among them. The Duke of Devonshire, who never tired of visiting the Crystal Palace, was often at Rockhills. Paxton had told him that he would always be welcome; and the Duke, taking him at his word, would sometimes arrive unexpectedly with a train of servants and stay for weeks on end. The Duke was growing old and was frequently ill; and he depended on Paxton more than ever.

Paxton himself was far from well; and the money troubles of the Crystal Palace had a bad effect on his health. He had hoped that Sarah would be with him at Rockhills; but Sarah had no love for the new house and she hated Sydenham and the Crystal Palace which took up so much of her husband's time. To her, Barbrook was home; and no other place was the equal of Chatsworth.

Sarah simply could not move with the times. She wanted her husband back at Chatsworth and everything to be as it had been in the past. All her life she had been reserved and retiring, and she could not change now. When her husband was at Chatsworth and sat at dinner with the Duke and his guests she stayed quietly at home. Although she came sometimes to Rockhills she hurried back to Chatsworth as soon as she could; and she still had work there to do. She was in fact so retiring that she had been Lady Paxton for five years before she would consent to appear at Court. She agreed to make her official curtsey to the Queen only when the Duke begged her to do so. The Duke, who had retained his deep respect for Sarah, arranged her presentation in style: Sarah was presented by his niece, the Duchess of Sutherland, who was Mistress of the Robes.

Paxton's first years at Rockhills were clouded with family troubles. George Paxton, growing wilder and more difficult as he grew older, was a constant worry to his parents. Then Laura, the daughter who was born while Paxton was on the Grand Tour with the Duke and had been packed off to school in Germany for corresponding with a boy, had an accident while still at school; and she died before her parents could reach her.

Sarah Paxton was overwhelmed by this sorrow; but she found some comfort in the affection of her other daughters. The elder girls were all grown up. They had plenty of admirers, and their parents hoped they would marry men who could afford to keep them in comfort. But the girls, who had been brought up to be independent, chose to marry for love. Paxton was not very pleased when Emily, his eldest daughter, informed him that she wanted to marry George Stokes, his architectural assistant. Stokes was his right-hand man; and when Paxton had recovered from his disappointment he realized that Emily had made a wise decision. He was devoted to all his daughters; and two of the older girls lived in London after they married and were often at Rockhills with him.

The two youngest girls, Rosa and Annie, were twelve

and ten years old when their father took Rockhills. While they were at school they spent most of their holidays at Chatsworth; but as they grew older they spent more time at Sydenham. Although in their late teens they were considered grown-up young ladies, they were as high-spirited and mischievous as they had been as children. In Victorian days young ladies were strictly supervised and were not allowed to walk in the streets of London alone. One day, however, Rosa and Annie escaped, hailed a hansom cab and drove down Regent Street. Another day Annie, who knew a great deal about horses, hired a two-horsed carriage, climbed on to the driver's seat and drove the carriage up St James's Street into Piccadilly. Their mother would have been horrified had she known of these exploits. She would have been still more horrified had she known that once, on holiday in Scarborough, Rosa and Annie had crept out of their hotel while she was in bed and asleep and gone to the theatre with friends.

The Paxton girls were all of them intelligent and good talkers. They were very fond of one another, and the younger girls got on well with their brothers-in-law. It was quite different with their only sister-in-law. George Paxton's wife was ignorant, vulgar and flaunting; and the girls found her utterly impossible. She was so pleased with herself for marrying the only son of an important man that she began to give herself airs and to patronize her sisters-in-law. She even had her handkerchiefs embroidered with a coronet although, as the daughter-in-law of a mere knight, she was not entitled to do anything of the sort.

Paxton and Sarah never discussed George and his wife in front of their daughters, but the girls knew very well that George was going steadily downhill. George only came to see his parents now when he wanted to borrow money. Paxton had decided that lending or giving money to George did no good: the money was immediately gambled away at cards or on horse races. But Sarah could never resist her son's pleas. She continued to send him money even though she knew only too well how it would be spent. She longed most desperately to be able to help him; and to the end of her life she went on hoping that he would reform.

CHAPTER NINE

Clouded Years

In 1854, a few weeks after the opening of the Sydenham Crystal Palace, Paxton had decided to stand for Parliament as Liberal candidate for the city of Coventry. Sarah was very much against it; and so were the friends who knew him best. One of them, John Ellis, Chairman of the Midland Railway, the man who had first encouraged him to go ahead with his designs for the Hyde Park Crystal Palace, wrote him an affectionate letter of warning.

"Here's Ellis telling me that my health won't stand it," cried Paxton to Sarah one morning when he opened the letter. "It's all stuff and nonsense. I'm only fifty-one, and there's nothing wrong with my health that hard work won't cure."

Sarah gave him a searching look. "Mr Ellis is perfectly right," she said. "You're doing far too much already; surely you must know that. If you insist on standing for Coventry you'll have to fight a hard election campaign. If you win it will only be the beginning of your troubles. Coventry's a rough place, a very rough place; and you'll have to meet all sorts of industrial troubles."

"All the more reason why I should represent

Coventry. Perhaps I shall be able to do something to improve conditions for the workers."

Sarah shook her head. "Besides," she added plaintively, "if you get into Parliament I shall never see you at Chatsworth at all."

Paxton assured her that he would often be at Chatsworth and that he would never neglect the Duke's concerns. He hoped that she would come more frequently to Rockhills; but he was well aware that although his sub-agents at Chatsworth were capable men Sarah's presence was necessary when he himself was away for any length of time.

Paxton was deeply grateful to his wife and so was the Duke; but Sarah was chiefly concerned to keep her husband at home and to prevent him from over-working.

"Chatsworth is so beautiful," she said, "and you're missing all the beauty. Sometimes I think you no longer care for Chatsworth, or for me. You care only for your own ambitions."

Paxton denied this. "A man must do what he thinks right," he said, "and I hope I shall be useful if I get into Parliament. I'm well aware that I have enough architectural work to keep me busy for years, to say nothing of my other commitments; but I should still have time to be a conscientious Member of Parliament."

Sarah was not convinced. She was desperately afraid that if he added to his burden he would ruin his health. But Paxton was an obstinate man and the warnings of Sarah and John Ellis went unheeded. In the end he entered Parliament without fighting an election campaign because no candidate was put up against him.

However, he fought and won later election campaigns, and he represented Coventry in Parliament for the rest of his parliamentary life.

Although he was not a fluent speaker Paxton made an admirable Member. He spoke seldom but always to the point; and he was highly respected for the soundness of his judgment. He was too independent minded to follow the Liberal policy line without question; and more than once he came into collision with the leaders of his Party.

Coventry, as Sarah had warned him, was not an easy constituency to represent. There was poverty and a great deal of unemployment among the workers; and industrial troubles led to strikes and lock-outs. One of the chief reasons for the distress and unemployment was the fact that most of the workers were employed as ribbon-makers. There was a big demand for ribbons which were widely used on women's clothes and as bonnet strings. There had been an import duty on French silks; but when this was lifted French-made ribbons could be bought in England more cheaply than English; and so English-made ribbons began to go out of fashion.

Paxton, who was deeply sympathetic with the troubles of the unemployed, was convinced that the only solution to the problem was to start up new industries and, at the same time, to improve the railway service so that trains could carry more goods. During the next few years a cotton mill was opened and a number of worsted and woollen mills; and Paxton launched a scheme by which the unemployed were given work clearing land and making a common.

In the meantime, the Crimean War had broken out between England, and her ally France, and Russia. The cause of the trouble was the Duke of Devonshire's old friend the Emperor Nicholas I. The Emperor wanted to extend Russia's influence in south-east Europe; and right up to the last minute people were hoping that war might be averted. Paxton was one of these people. He felt that one man, and one man only, could avert it: the Duke of Devonshire. He wrote to the Duke in February, 1854, begging him to go himself to Russia and intercede with the Emperor in the name of their long friendship. "The Emperor has never known the true state of feeling in France and England on the Eastern question," wrote Paxton, "but he will listen to your Grace."

The Duke was in Brighton at the time. "I have got your letter from Chatsworth," he replied. "It is now too late. The English bull-dog has been let loose, and it is not for me to stop him if I could."

Paxton was secretly relieved at the Duke's answer. The Duke was so often ill now and the journey, even in a comfortably fitted steamer, would have taxed his strength. All the same Paxton had felt that he should at least suggest a peace mission. It is most unlikely that the Duke would have succeeded; and in any event, as he said, it was too late. War was declared on March 28, 1854. A year later the Emperor died; but the war continued.

Everybody has heard of the muddle and confusion of the Crimean War, the ghastly sufferings of the troops, and the heroism of Florence Nightingale. At first things had seemed to be going well for Britain. During the autumn of 1854 the British Army won a victory; and the way lay open to Sevastopol, the chief Russian strong-hold in the Crimea, which must be captured if the war was to be won. The winter of 1854–5 was particularly severe. The soldiers who were preparing to march on Sevastopol suffered terribly from cold and sickness and thousands died. Tales of chaos and mismanagement began to filter through to London, and it soon became clear that something drastic must be done.

Paxton had his own ideas on the subject. In a speech he had made at Coventry before his election to Parliament he put forward an original scheme. He was not a soldier, and he knew nothing of Army affairs. But he was a practical man with some experience of engineering: he believed in railway development, and he realized that communications must play a big part in the successful siege of Sevastopol. Communications meant railways and roads. Railways and roads meant earthworks – the shifting of soil and so on. Paxton knew all about earthworks. He also knew all about the labourers, the "navigators" – or navvies as they were called – who worked for him at Sydenham and elsewhere. His idea was that gangs of navvies should be sent to the Crimea to help the Army build the earthworks.

The Times greeted Paxton's idea with enthusiasm. As a result the Government went part of the way, and commissioned a firm of contractors to make a railway between Balaklava and Sevastopol, a distance of six-and-a-half miles. Miners, carpenters, plate-layers and navvies were sent out from England to construct the railway, and they made a good job of it. But a railway by itself could not begin to cope with the immense task of carrying troops and supplies to the front line. The need was for a road, trenches, and other earthworks: without them the chaos continued, and the transport system broke down.

Paxton went on pressing the Government to form a permanent Corps of Navigators to do the necessary work. The Government hesitated; and Paxton spoke bitterly of the uncalled-for sufferings of the soldiers and of the incompetence of the Army authorities. *The Times* took up the cry. So, too, did the men who believed, as Paxton did, that the plight of the soldiers was caused to a large extent by the breakdown of transport.

In the spring of 1855 the Government at length decided to act. On April 24 Paxton received a letter from Lord Panmure, Secretary at War:

> Her Majesty's Government has decided upon forming a Corps of Navigators to be employed in the Crimea upon the duty of forming entrenchments and other earthworks. Your great experience in the employment of these workpeople marks you out as the person probably the best qualified to afford aid to Her Majesty's Government in the selection of persons to take charge of the superintendence and management of the Corps. I have accordingly the honour to request that you will favour me with any suggestions you may have to offer with respect to the formation and organization of the Corps.

Paxton was intensely relieved. Of course he was prepared to accept the Government's invitation: there was no question of that. But, after thinking the matter over, he made two conditions. The first was that he should be given a free hand to carry out the task "in a business-like manner, without unnecessary trouble in matters of mere detail". The second was that he should be offered no reward for his services: for he believed that a salary or any other kind of payment "would interfere with and weaken" his independence.

Lord Panmure agreed to Paxton's conditions. Paxton set to work. As he and others realized, the need was not only for roads and trenches but also for hospitals, huts and wells; and Paxton knew where to look for the best men to carry out the work. Large numbers of the work-men who had been busy making the grounds of the Sydenham Crystal Palace were now becoming free; and Paxton had a high opinion of them.

At Sydenham, he called the men together to explain what he had in mind. "The Government has put me in charge of a scheme to help the British soldiers in the Crimea," he told them. "As I see it, the soldier's job is to fight. Soldiers are trained to fight, but they are not trained to build. Your job, on the other hand, is to build and not to fight. You are trained builders; and I reckon that each one of you can do the building work of three unskilled soldiers. I'm looking for a thousand builders to volunteer for service in the Crimea. Before any of you decide to volunteer I should like you to ask me some questions."

"Will they make soldiers of us?" asked one man suspiciously.

"No, they certainly will not," answered Paxton

crisply. "You will be a civilian Corps, not an Army Corps. You will not wear uniform, and you will not be armed. You will be under the direction of your own officer, who will be called Chief Superintendent; and the Chief Superintendent will be answerable only to the Commander-in-Chief of the Army and the Chief Officer of the Royal Engineers. So you see, you will be a force on your own; and you will have your own equipment."

There was a pause. Then another man spoke. "What about pay, sir? I've a wife and eight children to keep."

"I was hoping somebody would ask me about pay," said Paxton. "You will be paid wages, very high wages, I may add, because the work will be very hard and the hours will be long. You won't be in danger like the soldiers; but you will have the satisfaction of helping yourselves and your families as well as your country." He paused. "Any more questions?"

"What will they call us?" the same man asked.

"The first idea was to call you the 'Corps of Navigators'," Paxton explained; "but the Government has now decided on the 'Army Works Corps'. Does that suit you?"

"That'll suit us fine, sir."

The men pressed forward; and Paxton realized thankfully that he would not be short of volunteers.

He was naturally tremendously enthusiastic about the scheme; and it came as a shock to learn that Lord Raglan, the Commander-in-Chief of the Army in the Crimea, and General Jones, the Commander of the Royal Engineers, were putting all sorts of difficulties in the way. General Jones wanted to increase his own force and not to rely on the Army Works Corps. And both he and Lord Raglan objected strongly to the employment of civilians who would be better paid than the troops. Besides, they argued, the soldiers had to risk their lives every minute of the day, while the navvies would not share the danger or be placed under the same strict discipline.

Paxton found it hard to understand that these arguments were really important. All he wanted was to strike a blow against the confusion at the front and the unnecessary sufferings of the troops. In his opinion, the Army Works Corps was the body to strike that blow; nothing else mattered.

Lord Raglan and General Jones had their misgivings; but they had to accept the Corps. Meanwhile, Paxton had appointed a most capable organizer as Chief Superintendent; and orders had been put in hand for the clothing and equipment of the thousand men who had been recruited. Paxton took the greatest interest in the men's comfort. He invented a special bell-shaped tent which would hold twenty-five men. The tent was equipped with a central pole of metal tubing which also formed the flue for a cooking stove. Another of his inventions was a bed of lightly framed angle iron which lifted a man above the ground and could be folded up when not in use. Paxton's tents, which were three or four times larger than the tents in general use, were thought to be a great improvement on the old pattern. Unfortunately he had reckoned without the howling gales of the Crimea, which tore his tents in pieces.

The first detachments of the Army Works Corps

arrived in the Crimea in August, 1855. Sevastopol fell the following month; and the need for roads to supplement the railway line between Balaklava and Sevastopol became more urgent than ever. As Lord Raglan had prophesied (he died before his prophecy came true) there was friction between the soldiers and the navvies, and a number of other troubles which were never

smoothed out. All the same, the navvies quickly got down to their work and soon proved their worth. As the war dragged on more navvies were recruited and sent to the Crimea; and Paxton reckoned that 5,000 more would be needed if the men were to face another winter. He bombarded the War Department until he won his case. Two thousand five hundred additional men were recruited, equipped, and shipped to the Crimea. But the Russians were defeated by the French and the Sardinians, who had joined them, before the remainder of the Army Works Corps was needed; and to everybody's relief war came to an end.

The Army Works Corps had cost the country a good deal of money. Many of the navvies had failed to come up to Paxton's high opinion of them. Yet, despite the troubles, the Corps did valuable work in road making and the building of hospitals, huts, depots and stores.

Paxton had spent a vast amount of energy in his efforts to make the Corps a success. He was worried and overtired; and yet, even when the war was over, there were still many loose ends to be tidied up. And all the time he was as busy as ever with his building and engineering schemes. In 1853 he had been made a Justice of the Peace, and, as always, he took his duties very seriously. He was more deeply involved than ever in railway development, overseas as well as at home; and in due course he became a director of the company which constructed Brunel's famous *Great Eastern*, the largest steamship of the day, which was chiefly used for the laying of cables under the Atlantic and the Mediterranean.

In the spring of 1855 a question had arisen in Parliament in which Paxton was extremely interested. The House of Commons set up a Committee to examine the problem of communications in London. London was growing very fast. Streams of people poured into the city every day by train, omnibus, river steamer, or on foot; and many of the streets were becoming choked with traffic. The Committee agreed that something must be done without delay to control the traffic and prevent the confusion from spreading. A number of suggestions were discussed. One of them was to construct new roads and to widen existing roads. Another was to link by rail the main stations, the docks, the River Thames, and the General Post Office, in an effort to keep people and goods away from the streets. A third suggestion concerned the Metropolitan Railway, which was just about to be started: it involved the connection of various districts of London by means of underground lines.

Paxton had his own ideas on the subject. In June, 1855, he was invited to give evidence before the Committee; and he was listened to with respect.

"It is clear," said Paxton, who had gone into the problem thoroughly, "that the railways ought to be connected in some way. This would deal to some extent both with goods and passenger traffic. But I have here a plan which would enable large numbers of people to travel to their destination without using the streets at all."

His words caused some surprise. "Has your plan something to do with glass?" enquired one member cautiously.

Paxton smiled. "As you know, I have a weakness for glass," he said; "but then, gentlemen, I am convinced that we haven't even begun to exhaust the usefulness of glass in building." He unrolled the papers which he held in his hand. "These," he added, "are my designs for a Grand Girdle Railway and Boulevard under Glass."

"A very imposing title, Sir Joseph! Will you be so good as to explain your idea to us?" said the Chairman.

"With the greatest pleasure," said Paxton. "My girdle would encircle the Metropolis with a boulevard – or arcade – built of iron and roofed with glass. It would start at the Royal Exchange, cross the river at Rotherhithe by a special bridge, pass through Lambeth, cross the river again at Westminster; and then pass through the districts of Victoria, Chelsea, Kensington, Notting Hill and Paddington to Islington; and from Islington it would return full circle to the Royal Exchange. The total length of the girdle would be $11\frac{1}{2}$ miles; and this would include a branch from just south of the river to the north behind Piccadilly Circus."

Paxton paused to see the effect of his words. Several members nodded and there were murmurs of approval; and he went on more confidently. "My design is for an arcade with a vaulted roof, which would be 108 feet at the highest point. The arcade would be constructed much in the same style as the Crystal Palace, but there would be certain alterations and improvements. No paintwork would be needed, for instance: Staffordshire tiles with burnt-in colouring could be used to take the place of ordinary woodwork. On the lower level of the arcade there would be houses and shops connected by an enclosed corridor, or road. At a higher level, on each side of the arcade, there would be a railway. There would be eight railway lines in all, four for express trains, four for stopping trains, to enable people to alight at any point. This would mean that communication would be simple inside the arcade. It would also enable people to reach their destination in record time. I reckon, gentlemen, that the distance between any two points could be covered by train in fifteen minutes; and if necessary my railways could be directly connected with the main line stations."

"How about ventilation?" enquired a member.

"I have had some experience of ventilating buildings," replied Paxton, "from the smallest glasshouse to the largest – the Crystal Palace. As I have managed, successfully I believe, to ventilate all these buildings I am satisfied that I could ventilate my arcade in such a way that the atmosphere inside it would be pure and free from the smoke of the city."

Paxton knew far more about the problems of ventilation than any member of the Committee; and members were content to take his word for it. They were also most impressed to see that he had designed his girdle in such a way that it would not run parallel with any of the main streets and that it would not be necessary to knock down any valuable property in order to install it.

"How much do you think such a scheme as yours would cost?" Paxton was asked.

"I doubt if it could be carried out for much less than £3½ millions," Paxton admitted. "If the job is to be done it should be done properly; and naturally the rents from the houses and shops and the railway fares would pay back much of the original sum."

Paxton himself was in love with his idea. To his joy, the Committee recommended to the House of Commons "the evidence and splendid designs of Sir Joseph Paxton".

Paxton's designs for the Great Victorian Way – as the girdle came to be called – also appealed strongly to the Prince Consort. At the Prince's request, Paxton described his plans in detail. The Queen, too, was interested; and summoned Paxton to Windsor to explain them to her. The plans were then put on view in the House of Lords. Among the people who went to look at them was the Duke of Devonshire. He was filled with wonder and admiration at such a marvel.

In the end Paxton's scheme came to nothing; for the House of Commons refused to accept it. The scheme was vast and unusual, too unusual and too expensive to meet with approval. Paxton was bitterly disappointed at the decision. The dream of a London encircled by a crystal arcade had been with him for two years. The scheme sounds fantastic today; but it was much brighter and more exciting than the plan which was finally adopted, of constructing a passenger railway underground.

Paxton never allowed disappointment to sour him. If one scheme failed there were plenty more; and he was as much in demand as ever as an architect, engineer and railway expert. However busy he might be he was always ready to lay aside all his work when the Duke of Devonshire sent for him. The Duke, now elderly and ill, became more and more restless as he grew older. He was often at Rockhills, with Dr Condell and a train of servants; he was sometimes at Brighton, at Chatsworth or one or other of his houses, or at Lismore in Ireland. And wherever the Duke might be Paxton had to be ready to follow at a minute's notice.

In January, 1858, the Duke was at Hardwick. Paxton, who was with him, had business to do for the Duke at Bolton Abbey, and came to say goodbye to him on the morning of Saturday, January 16. He found the Duke seated in a wheeled chair, looking quite well but rather anxious and depressed.

"I am worried about the pictures in the great gallery, Paxton," said the Duke fretfully. "They ought to be rehung and we've done nothing at all about it."

"Shall I ask an expert for some advice, your Grace? Mr Peter Cunningham's the man. He would give you any help and advice you needed."

The Duke brightened. "An excellent idea," he said. "I knew you would think of something, Paxton."

"I'll write to him now before I leave, shall I?"

"Please do."

Paxton sat down at a writing table. "Goodbye, your Grace," he said when he had finished the letter. "I shan't be away long. I shall finish my business and be back here on Thursday."

"Remember Thursday," said the Duke, more to himself than to Paxton. "Very probably you will find me gone when you return," he added.

"Gone? To Brighton, your Grace?" Paxton knew that Dr Condell thought that the Duke would be better in Brighton than in Derbyshire during the winter months.

As though in answer the Duke picked up a copy of *Punch* which was lying on the table beside him, and pointed to the caricature of two old men who were talking about superstition. One of the old men was saying to the other: "Well, thank God, I am not superstitious, but I don't like thirteen to dinner."

Paxton was well aware of the superstition that if thirteen people sat down to dinner together one of them would die before the end of the year. In fact, the previous evening, owing to a mistake on the Duke's part, there had been thirteen to dinner. Paxton had offered to ask Sarah to come and make a fourteenth; but the Duke had laughingly refused. The superstition was nonsense, he insisted. All the same, Paxton had been uneasy throughout the evening. Now, however, he realized that the Duke, too, was uneasy; but he felt he must do nothing which might alarm him. So he simply shrugged his shoulders, laughed, and left the room, promising once again to be back on Thursday.

The Duke was busy for the rest of the day examining the pictures in the great gallery. In the evening he dined quietly with Dr Condell and Mr Cottingham, his sub-agent. After dinner the three men sat in the drawing-room, a beautiful room hung with tapestries and pictures.

Suddenly the Duke sat up very straight in his wheeled chair and pointed a finger at the fireplace.

"Did you not see two female figures pass just now and stop at the fireplace?" he asked wonderingly.

"I saw nothing, your Grace," replied the doctor briskly. "It was just your fancy."

The Duke shook his head. "Strange," he murmured, "very strange!"

Although Dr Condell had made light of the incident he was startled and a little scared. But the Duke did not refer to it again. Next morning he asked to be wheeled again into the picture gallery and spent another morning planning where the portraits might be rehung. "I should like my portrait to be placed near my mother's," he said softly as one of his servants wheeled him away.

After dinner the Duke asked for some music. A musician, who, like the doctor, was a member of the household, came to the drawing-room to play the piano for him. The Duke, wrapped in a plaid shawl, had his chair placed close to the piano; and he sat listening, occasionally beating time to the music, until the Doctor came to help him to bed. Some time during the night the old man died peacefully in his sleep.

CHAPTER TEN

Return to Chatsworth

The Duke of Devonshire's heir, Lord Burlington, was a distant cousin. Apart from his sisters the Duke had had no near relations; and although Lord Burlington and his family had looked on him as a friend they were not deeply attached to him. His closest friend, as they knew, was Joseph Paxton; and Paxton would grieve for the Duke far more deeply than they would.

Paxton had no time to give way to grief. As soon as he heard the news he came hurrying back from Bolton. There he met Lord Burlington; and Lord Burlington, who knew that this was what his cousin would have wished, asked Paxton to take full charge of the arrangements for the funeral. The Duke had left instructions that he would like to be buried in Edensor churchyard. His coffin was therefore taken to Chatsworth by night, Paxton riding alone behind it.

At Chatsworth Paxton flung himself into the business of sending instructions about trains and carriages to the Duke's relatives. He was far too busy to think much of his own feelings. It was only as he followed the long line of family mourners to the graveside that he was stricken with the knowledge of all he had lost.

In the days that followed he had time to relive his life

at Chatsworth from the far-off day at Chiswick when the
Duke had invited the inexperienced gardener to be
superintendent of the grounds at Chatsworth. He could
look back on all the triumphs he and the Duke had
shared: the search for rare plants: the Emperor Fountain; the Great Conservatory; the Lily House and many
more. He could think of the Duke's admiration for the
Crystal Palace, and for all his other schemes. Without
the Duke's generosity and encouragement none of these
things would have been possible; but, to Paxton, the
greatest of all the Duke's gifts had been his trust and
friendship. There was no one now to take pride in his
schemes; no one to whom he was necessary, as he had
been to the Duke. In the past he had been able to rely
on Sarah, with her wisdom and understanding. But as
she grew older Sarah was becoming more and more
withdrawn; and Paxton, always occupied with one
scheme or other, had done nothing to bridge the gap
which was widening between them.

For days after the funeral Paxton was too lost in grief
and apathy to give any thought to the future. But Sarah,
who also grieved for the Duke, was beginning to worry.
She was frightened about her husband's health, and
afraid that if the new Duke decided to engage another
agent she and her husband would be turned out of their
home.

One morning Mr Currey, the Duke's lawyer, came to
Barbrook at Lord Burlington's request to discuss plans
for the future. He was shocked to see how ill and old
Paxton was looking, and well aware that he himself
had been sent on a difficult errand. Lord Burlington had

known for some time that once again his cousin was spending far too much money on Chatsworth and that his estates were encumbered by debt. Severe economy would be necessary if the estates were to be freed from this burden; and this would mean that some of Paxton's most cherished schemes would have to go. Lord Burlington shrank from the idea of asking Paxton to destroy any of his own work; and he wanted to appoint an agent of his own. But no power on earth would persuade him to dismiss the man who had done so much for his cousin. Currey had come to put the idea into Paxton's head that he should offer to resign.

If Paxton had not been so distraught he would have thought of this himself: but now, it needed only a hint from the old lawyer to bring him to his senses. He decided to ask Lord Burlington for an immediate interview and to take on himself the responsibility of resigning.

The next morning he called at the big house and handed Lord Burlington a letter of resignation. Lord Burlington, who dreaded the prospect of causing Paxton further pain, was impressed by his quiet dignity. He wrote an answer which Paxton received three days later. In his letter Lord Burlington accepted his resignation, thanked him for his thirty-two years of devoted service at Chatsworth and for all he had done in the past. "It is my wish and hope," he concluded, "that you should still continue to live in the house at Chatsworth which has so long been your home, and which must be endeared to you by so many recollections."

Paxton replied at once, thanking the Duke for his

kindness and accepting his generous offer. Sarah was overjoyed that she need never leave Barbrook; and she was delighted when the Duke invited Paxton to act, not as agent, but as an adviser.

The two men soon learned to respect and like one another; and when Paxton was at Chatsworth he was invited to dine at the big house as he had been in the old Duke's day.

But everything was different now, different, and to Paxton, very sad. He understood the need for strict economy; but he was most upset when a large number of the estate workers were dismissed, and their unhappiness merely added to his own. He did his utmost to find work for the men elsewhere; but they did not want to move, and suitable jobs were not always easy to find.

For Sarah, life was somewhat easier. She could now hand over her part of the estate business to a successor, and she was thankful to be rid of the burden of bills, accounts and monthly payments which she had carried for so long. Paxton persuaded her to spend more time at Rockhills; and she travelled abroad several times, something she had never had time to do before. She still helped and advised her husband with his many business affairs; and her advice was as good as ever; and she had a new interest in her grandchildren as they arrived. But Barbrook remained her home; and she was never really happy anywhere but at Chatsworth.

The Duke and his daughter, who acted as his hostess, were friendly and kind. Sarah appreciated their kindness and was glad to see them when they called on her;

but she refused to break her old rule and remained quietly in the background.

Paxton was not very often at Chatsworth. It was too full of memories; and he could not reconcile himself to all the changes. The only cure he knew for unhappiness and depression was work, and still more work; and the next few years were as crowded as ever. He was still working for the Rothschild family; and Ferrières, the mansion he had designed in France for Baron James de Rothschild, caused him a great deal of trouble. On one occasion he had to drop everything else and hurry over to France to intervene in a quarrel which had broken out between the English and French workmen. This trip was one of a number of business trips to Europe. In 1854 Paxton had been to Paris at the request of the Emperor Napoleon III to show him the plans of the Sydenham Crystal Palace. The following year, when the Emperor saw the Palace for himself, he was so fascinated by it that he decided that France must have a Crystal Palace at St Cloud, near Paris. Later, Paxton returned to France with designs for a truly magnificent glass building. Unfortunately, his designs were considered too costly; and another plan, far less splendid, was chosen.

Paxton was still convinced that glass had a great future, and in his later years he was experimenting with a combination of glass and other materials. He used vitreous tiles – glass fused on metal; and slate as well as wood and iron. He was also more concerned with the actual needs of the areas in which his buildings were to stand. The Sydenham Crystal Palace, for example, was much more suited to its environment than the original in Hyde Park. In the same way, his designs for a "Crystal Sanitarium", an exercise room for the London Chest Hospital, were carefully drawn to suit the layout of the Hospital. The Crystal Sanitarium was never built. Other ambitious schemes which came to nothing included a plan to cover the open court of the Royal Exchange with glass; and one for a Crystal Palace in New York. In his later work Paxton owed much to the skill and knowledge of his son-in-law George Stokes; but he remained the mind behind each new venture. The work of his last years included designs for two public parks in Scotland, one at Dundee and one at Dunfermline; and a garden near the Bois de Boulogne in Paris. In other parks, gardens and buildings his designs were used in part.

Railway affairs took up as much of Paxton's time as ever; and these also involved him in long and tiring journeys to the Continent. His railway interests brought him in touch with Charles Markham, at that time Locomotive Superintendent of the Midland Railway. Markham, a dark, bearded man, with an abrupt manner, fell in love with Rosa Paxton, who was fifteen years his junior. The Paxtons had hoped for a brilliant marriage for their gay and charming daughter; but Rosa, who was now twenty-two and very much in love, refused to listen to any objections. She married Charles Markham in 1862; and the marriage was exceedingly happy.

At the time of Rosa's marriage Paxton was hoping for the fulfilment of one of his dearest wishes – the construction of a through railway line to Manchester.

Unfortunately he did not live to see it. Meanwhile, he plunged more deeply than ever into work. He was still very active in the House of Commons; and although he spoke seldom he was busy behind the scenes with every scheme in which his experience could be of use. He advised on matters concerning St James's Park and the Serpentine, for example. He was particularly interested in the future of shipping and the development of waterways. He was a promoter of the Thames Graving Dock; and he spoke forcibly in the House of Commons in favour of building more iron ships. He was Chairman of the House of Commons Committee which recommended a plan for the drainage and development of the Thames Embankment. A suggestion had been made for the Low Level Sewer to be carried along the Strand. Paxton opposed this idea; and he persuaded the Committee that the only place for the sewer was along the foreshore of the Thames and within the Embankment itself. This idea was adopted when the plans for the Victoria Embankment were finally accepted; but Paxton was no longer living when the Embankment was completed. His knowledge of drainage was of value to another House of Commons Committee – the Select Committee on the Sewage of Towns. In his evidence, he described the successful experiments he had made at Chatsworth so long before in the use of sewage as a fertilizer.

Plans had been on foot for some time to hold a second International Exhibition in 1862. Trade was bad, and many people were opposed to the idea. Paxton was among them; but on this occasion he was not consulted.

The death of the Prince Consort in 1861 was a shatter-
ing blow to the Queen. It also deprived the organizers
of the Exhibition of his wisdom and vast experience.
They decided to go ahead with the Exhibition, which
was held in a large brick building that had cost £320,000
to erect, a far larger sum than the Crystal Palace.
Paxton described the building as "a beast". He was
probably feeling sore because nobody had asked his
advice. But other people also found the building
hideously ugly: they pointed out that it was not only
inferior to but far more expensive than the Crystal
Palace, and they were not surprised when it failed to
pay its way.

One of Paxton's final ventures took him back to the
scenes of his boyhood. He was invited to design a house
for the owner of Battlesden Park in Bedfordshire, where
once he had worked as a gardener's boy. The old house,
when he took George Stokes to inspect it, had fallen
almost into a ruin. Paxton had ideas for rebuilding; but
in the end it was Stokes who undertook the work.
Paxton's health was far from good; but he refused to
give in. He had long been interested in the Volunteer
Movement in Derbyshire; and, as though to prove that
there was nothing wrong with him, he joined the
Matlock Rifles at the age of fifty-eight, and appeared on
parade in uniform and sword.

Several of his friends now began to suggest to him that
he should give up his parliamentary seat at Coventry
and stand for a constituency with fewer industrial problems. This he refused to do; but in the spring of 1865
he decided to quit Parliament altogether. He was not an

old man – only sixty-two; but he had come to the end of his tether.

Paxton himself sensed that he had not long to live. If he could not work and plan he was content to be with his family, and he adored his grandchildren. One of his favourites, a little girl named Geraldine, used to practise her dancing to amuse him. "I have got a musical

box with twelve tunes," wrote Paxton to the child's mother; "it will drive Geraldine wild."

Friends were still welcome at Rockhills; but too much talking tired him. One day the Duke of Devonshire's daughter and her sister-in-law called and they were alarmed to find him so ill and feeble.

Towards the end of May, 1865, a flower show was held at the Crystal Palace. Paxton, who was determined to be present, was too weak to walk and had to be wheeled in a chair. As he entered the building friends and acquaintances flocked about him, all eager to talk to him and enquire after his health. But he was so exhausted that he had to give up before the tour of the building was completed. He was wheeled home and went straight to bed; and he did not get up again.

During the next few days the weather stayed warm and sunny; and Whit Monday was brilliant.

"I am so glad it is fine for the people's holiday," murmured Paxton as he lay in bed gazing out of the windows at the sunshine which streaked his lawns. Then he slept a little; woke up; and slept again. He was well aware that he was dying; and at dawn on June 8 he slipped quietly away.

His body was taken back to Chatsworth; and his grave was dug in Edensor churchyard, near the grave of his friend and master. The seventh Duke and his brothers and many of Paxton's friends attended the funeral.

▣   ▣   ▣

Today, just over a hundred years since Paxton's death, it is clear that a good deal of his work was over-praised in his lifetime. Some of his most spectacular triumphs, which gave pleasure to so many people, have long since vanished. The Great Conservatory at Chatsworth, which had never been run economically, was doomed to destruction in the difficult years which followed the World War of 1914–18. The Conservatory had been made to last; and in 1923, after no fewer than five attempts to blow it up had failed, Rosa Markham's engineer son Charles was called in to advise. By a stroke of irony it was Paxton's grandson who succeeded in bringing the Conservatory to the ground with dynamite.

The Sydenham Crystal Palace had a longer life. In 1867 a fire destroyed the north transept with the famous Egyptian Court which was never rebuilt. By 1914 the building was bankrupt; but after the War it was bought for the nation, re-opened by King George V and Queen Mary, and given a new lease of life. On November 30, 1936, there was another fire; and the mighty glass and iron building, which had withstood time and the weather for eighty-two years, shot up in flames and perished.

Paxton, of course, will always be remembered as the architect of the Crystal Palace, which brought glamour and magic into the lives of millions of people. Yet he probably did his finest work as a gardener – particularly as a landscape gardener – and as a designer of greenhouses. The many rare plants which he cultivated, and the gardens and parks which he designed, all prove that in his own line he was a genius.

There is something else, too, for which he deserves to be remembered. The famous man who had started life as a gardener's boy never failed to do everything he could to improve conditions for the poor and underprivileged. He was honest and sincere; simple yet dignified; and the warmth and kindliness of his personality gained him friends in every walk of life. As he lay dying he whispered a few words which reflect the whole of his life: "I am glad to think there is no one alive that I could not shake by the hand."

Book List

CHADWICK, GEORGE F. *The Works of Sir Joseph Paxton*, The Architectural Press, London (1961).

FFRENCH, YVONNE *The Great Exhibition*, 1851, Harvill (1950)

MARKHAM, VIOLET R. *Paxton and the Bachelor Duke*, Hodder & Stoughton (1935)

Index